Architectural
Drawing
in Virginia
1819-1969

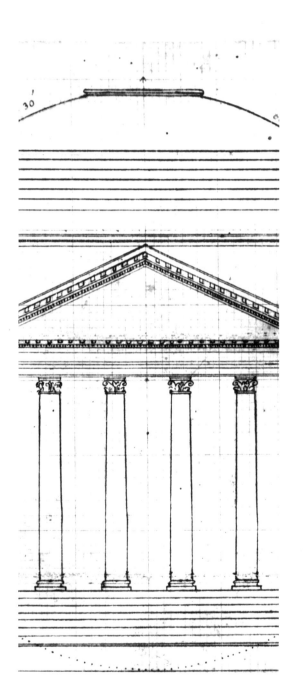

Architectural
Drawing
in Virginia
1819-1969

Exhibition and
Catalogue by

William B. O'Neal

School of Architecture
University of Virginia

Virginia Museum

School of Architecture
University of Virginia
October 18-26, 1969

Virginia Museum
November 3-30, 1969

For

Stanislaw John Makielski
who taught at the School of Architecture,
University of Virginia,
from its founding in 1919
until his retirement in 1964

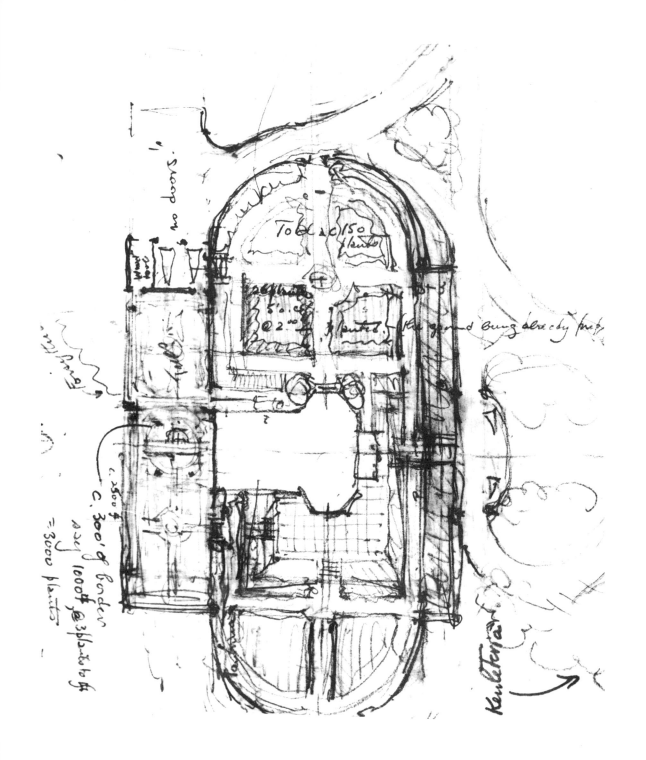

Contents

Foreword ix

Compiler's Note xi

Acknowledgments xii

Catalogue 1

Index 151

Foreword

One of the major values of any exhibition which surveys past accomplishments is that in providing a view of what is history a clearer, more precise direction toward the future can be shown. Such is one purpose of this recording of some of the past 150 years of architecture as practiced in Virginia. It is entirely appropriate in this year 1969, when the University celebrates the 150th year of its founding and the School of Architecture the 50th year of its beginning, that we take a comprehensive look at the forces and directions of architecture in Virginia. Perhaps the most striking facts to be noted in this exhibition are the great variety of styles and projects which have commanded the attention of architects employed in the state and the diversity of training and background of the architects who have worked in Virginia.

This is a time when all of the schools which comprise the University are making a special effort to provide excellence and leadership for the future and to collaborate effectively through interdisciplinary studies in searching for solutions to the many complex problems facing our society. The role of the School of Architecture is to train those who will help design the physical environment which will recognize in an orderly way the myriad of disciplines and facets of our life. It is especially interesting therefore to note that architects working in Virginia in the past concerned themselves not only with building but with such diverse projects as bridges and chairs and even railway carriages. They attempted to give order and quality to all aspects of the man-made environment. Such is the task of today's architect. He cannot concern himself only with the project on his drawing board, for its success will be dependent on his willingness and ability to adopt the broad view. The wide range of background of the architects who have worked in Virginia has brought to the state a cosmopolitan outlook and far from provincial approach. Recognition today and in the future of the role those from outside Virginia can play in assisting the progress of architecture within the state is another important lesson to be learned from this exhibition.

The organization and preparation of this exhibition is in itself an example of cooperation, for it has been prepared by the Virginia Museum and the School of Architecture, each contributing from its particular resources and talents.

This brief statement would be incomplete without a comment on the dedication of this catalogue. Stanislaw John Makielski (d. 1969) was intimately concerned and connected with the School of Architecture during almost all his adult life. He was one of the first graduates of the school and remained to serve as a distinguished teacher. The fact that he taught in almost every area of study within the school—from the precise discipline of structure to water-color painting—is evidence of his breadth of interest and ability. In honoring Mr. Makielski through this catalogue emphasis for the future is additionally placed on the necessity for diversity, broad vision, and concern by architects.

J. NORWOOD BOSSERMAN
Dean, School of Architecture
University of Virginia

Compiler's Note

Jefferson's university did not establish the school of architecture he had proposed until 1919, a century after the charter of the University of Virginia was granted. During the fifty years after that time the School of Architecture operated in various remodeled quarters, but now at last a building has been designed for its needs. To celebrate the 150th anniversary of the University of Virginia, the 50th anniversary of the School of Architecture, and the opening of the School's new building, the present exhibition was assembled.

The exhibition's time span (1819-1969) and its geographic limitations (Virginia) in no way limit its scope, for many nationally important architects have been associated with the Commonwealth during these years. The difficulty was to find, not the names, but the drawings, and it is inevitable that certain gaps exist in the exhibition itself.

Notable among these gaps is the lack of drawings by the following men who have either worked or taught in Virginia: Alvar Aalto; Simon Bernard; William Lawrence Bottomley; Marcel Breuer; Felix Candela; Carrère and Hastings; Cram, Ferguson, and Goodhue; John Haviland; Harrison and Abramovitz; Philip Johnson; Vincent Kling; Robert E. Lee; Ludwig Mies van der Rohe; Richard Neutra; John Russell Pope; Eero Saarinen; William Small; Thomas Stewart; Edward D. Stone; The Architects Collaborative; Henry van de Velde; and Ammi B. Young. For many, but valid, reasons it proved impossible to obtain drawings by any of them for the exhibition.

The beginning date of 1819 for the exhibition precluded the use of drawings by William Buckland, Benjamin Henry Latrobe, Robert Mills, Dr. William Thornton, and even George Washington.

Even the most cursory glance at this catalogue will show a preponderance of nineteenth-century drawings instead of a more even distribution through the almost equal time spans in both the nineteenth and twentieth centuries. There are two reasons for this.

In assembling this exhibition it was discovered that nineteenth-century architecture in Virginia, although full of interest and vitality, had been, after 1826, largely ignored, except for some of the work in Richmond. Since some rather rich stores of nineteenth-century drawings were uncovered during the period of research, it was felt that as much of this firsthand material should be presented as possible.

The inclusion of the nineteenth-century material inevitably left less space for the drawings of the twentieth century. But another very curious fact emerged. If nineteenth-century architecture was largely unrecorded after 1826, that of the twentieth century, well recorded as it is, showed far more carelessness in the matter of preserving drawings. The choice, then, was not as wide for the twentieth century despite the fact that a greater number of buildings of importance were erected after 1900 than before that date.

The University of Virginia itself quite rightly dominates the exhibition and the catalogue. Jefferson's own drawings are so rarely seen that the commemorative nature of the occasion provides the excuse for showing a group of them. It then follows that the drawings for the two other versions of the Rotunda should be shown. And, finally, it is appropriate that the very beautiful drawing for the School of Architecture building should be used to close the exhibition.

The most interesting discoveries during the course of the research were made at the Virginia State Library, where a group of competition drawings for the Washington Monument in Richmond survive, and here at the University of Virginia, where so many of the drawings of Alfred Landon Rives have been preserved. Both groups illuminate aspects of the nineteenth-century architectural world which are not very well known. The competition drawings have a wider range in quality and numbers of architects than one would have thought possible in America of 1849. The Rives drawings, on the other hand, show the meticulous care with which a student was trained in mid-nineteenth-century France and the uses to which that training was later put.

The unrecorded Strickland drawings, found in the Rives papers, are perhaps the most unexpected treasure of the exhibition. Their draughtsmanship and their crisp design place them at a very high level indeed.

But the level of draughtsmanship was high throughout the century and a half covered by the exhibition. And it is certainly striking that architects, who must deal in realities, have over so long a period presented their designs with so much care, ability, and imagination.

WILLIAM B. O'NEAL
University of Virginia
1969

Acknowledgments

The kindness of the many people who helped with the assembling of this exhibition and catalogue was far beyond either duty or civility. Their number is much too great for them to be named here, but their aid is no less appreciated because of that. The most profound thanks of the School of Architecture and of the compiler go out to them.

The generous lenders to the exhibition have made it possible, and they, too, are sent the most grateful thanks of the School of Architecture of the University of Virginia and of the compiler. Their names follow:

Avery Library, Columbia University
Brown University
City of Richmond
Mr. Thomas W. S. Craven
Mr. Kenneth De May
The Historical Society of Pennsylvania
The New-York Historical Society
Mr. and Mrs. Richard T. Pratt
The Royal Institute of British Architects
The University of Virginia
The Valentine Museum
The Virginia Military Institute
The Virginia National Bank
The Virginia State Library
Williams and Tazewell and Associates
Mr. Marcellus Wright, Jr.

Architectural
Drawing
in Virginia
1819-1969

Thomas Jefferson
1743-1826

Charlottesville, Virginia: University of Virginia, Pavilion II, 1819 (elevation and basement, first-floor, and second-floor plans)

12 1/4″ x 10 1/8″, pen and brown ink on co-ordinate paper

Scale: 1 inch equals 10 feet

Inscribed, upper left: Pavilion No. II Eastern range. Ionic of Fortuna Virilis

Notes on drawing, at left of elevation:

> this pediment is
> by mistake 10 f high
> instead of 8 f 10 2/3
> joists
> cieling [*sic*]
> bottom (?) entabl.
>   floor
> joists
>   cieling
> floor
>   cieling
> zocle
> floor

Specifications on reverse

Erasures occur around the chimneys of the first and basement floors; around the chimney in the northwest room on the second floor; and around a note at the right of the elevation

Laminated in plastic

Owned by the University of Virginia

Ex coll.: Dr. Wilson Cary Nicholas Randolph, by descent

Thomas Jefferson's lifelong interest in architecture reached a climax in his designs for the University of Virginia. Although building operations had begun in 1817 at the site of what had been first known as Albemarle Academy, secondly as Central College, and lastly as the University of Virginia, the year of the University's charter, 1819, was also the year the designs for the pavilions for East Lawn were executed.

Jefferson wrote the University's proctor, Arthur S. Brockenborough, on June 5, 1819, "As it is but lately concluded to commence the Eastern range of pavilions, & Dormitories I have not prepared the plans, nor shall I be at leisure to turn to that business till the week after the ensuing one." In another letter to the proctor on June 27, 1819, he noted that a meeting with him "would be attended by the receiving from me the plans of the Eastern range of Pavilions which I have now prepared and which may need explanation before I leave home for Bedford."

The drawings for the pavilions on the east, then, were prepared between June 12 and June 27, 1819, in Jefferson's seventy-seventh year.

The order for Pavilion II, as is noted on the drawing, is the Ionic of Fortuna Virilis. In his letter of April 16, 1821, giving the specifications for the capitals for the pavilion, he said:

Ionic capitels for columns whose lower diam. is 30. I. & dimind. diam. 26 1/2 to be copied from those of the temple of Fortuna virilis in Palladio. Observing that the two middle capitels show volutes in front and back and balusters in their flanks and the two corner capitels are what he calls angular, that is to say presenting Volutes in their front & outer flank. see Palladio. B. IV. Ch. 13. pa. 65. plate 37. Leoni's London edition.

Earlier in the same letter he describes this edition as "Leoni's edition publd. in London 1721," which was the second edition of Leoni's translation of Palladio.

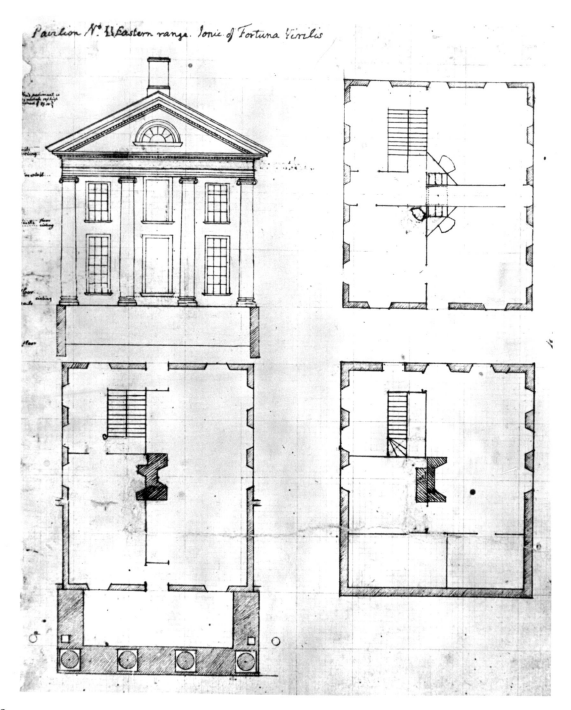

3

Thomas Jefferson

Charlottesville, Virginia: Pavilion IV, University of Virginia, 1819 (elevation and basement, first-floor and second-floor plans)

11 7/8" x 8 11/16", pen and brown ink on coordinate paper

Scale: 1 inch equals 10 feet

Inscribed, upper left: Pavilion No. IV. East. Doric of Albano.

Specifications on reverse

Laminated in plastic

Owned by the University of Virginia

Ex coll.: Dr. Wilson Cary Nicholas Randolph, by descent

Jefferson derived the "Doric of Albano" from Plate IV of Fréart de Chambray, *Parallele de l'architecture* (Paris, 1766), a book which he had known for a very long time. That text said of this order:

This rare masterpiece was found at Albano . . . among several other old and very curious fragments of architecture. . . . What I estime particularly in this is the grandeur of its majestic manner. . . . What is most fitting to be remarked & admired in this composition is the richness & the extraordinary form of the modillions . . . which produce a marvelous effect which is then still more augmented by the . . . crown mold, having made the Order seem gigantic: and it is properly this which one calls the grand manner (pp. 28-29).

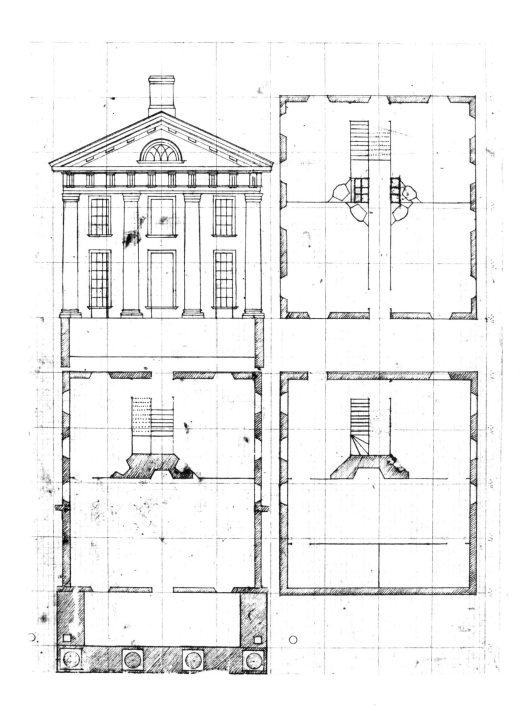

5

Thomas Jefferson

Charlottesville, Virginia: Pavilion VI, University of Virginia, 1819 (elevation and basement, first-floor and second-floor plans)

10 13/16″ x 8 9/16″, pen and brown ink on co-ordinate paper

Scale: 1 inch equals 10 feet

Inscribed, upper left: No. VI. East

Specifications on reverse

The first-floor and second-floor plans show the erasure of a portico.

Laminated in plastic

Owned by the University of Virginia

Ex coll.: Dr. Wilson Cary Nicholas Randolph, by descent

On the reverse of this drawing the order is indicated as the "Ionic of the theatre of Marcellus." The order applies, of course, only to the entablature, since there are no portico and consequently no columns for this pavilion, the one-story colonnade of the dormitories being carried across its façade.

The details of the entablature were derived from Plate XVI of Fréart de Chambray, who states in his text:

I have considered that the grandeur of the entablature, joined to its extraordinary simplicity may be a particular effect of the discretion of the Architect, who wished to place this Order on a very large building, & in a quite high place (p. 50).

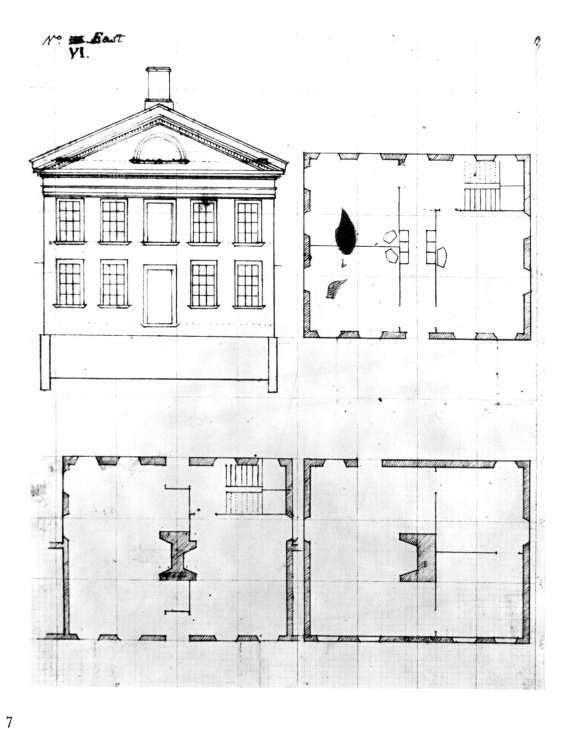

Thomas Jefferson

Charlottesville, Virginia: Pavilion VIII, University of Virginia, 1819 (elevation and basement, first-floor and second-floor plans)
11 1/2" x 8 5/8", pen and brown ink on coordinate paper
Scale: 1 inch equals 10 feet
Inscribed, upper left: No. VIII East. Corinthian. Diocletian's Baths.
Specifications on reverse
The elevation is drawn on a separate, small sheet of coordinate paper which has been pasted on the larger sheet.
Laminated in plastic
Owned by the University of Virginia
Ex coll.: Dr. Wilson Cary Nicholas Randolph, by descent

The specifications for this pavilion in Jefferson's notebook marked "Operations at and for the College" are headed "Latrobe's Lodge front. wings 9 f each, lodge 20 f=38 f. front." From this notation we may suppose that the design derived from a suggestion by Benjamin Henry Latrobe, who sent Jefferson some now-lost drawings during the fall of 1817.

The order was taken from Plate XXXIII of Fréart de Chambray where it was described as follows:

After this example of Corinthian, it is not at all necessary to search longer for the rich in Architecture, but it does not seem judicious to put it into execution, for the abundance of ornaments is not always estimable nor advantageous in an edifice: on the contrary . . . it is never necessary to indulge in profusion because . . . it gives birth, among the members, to a confusion which wounds the eye of the savant and which is antipathetic to the name of Order. One should, then, employ it only on great public works (p. 79).

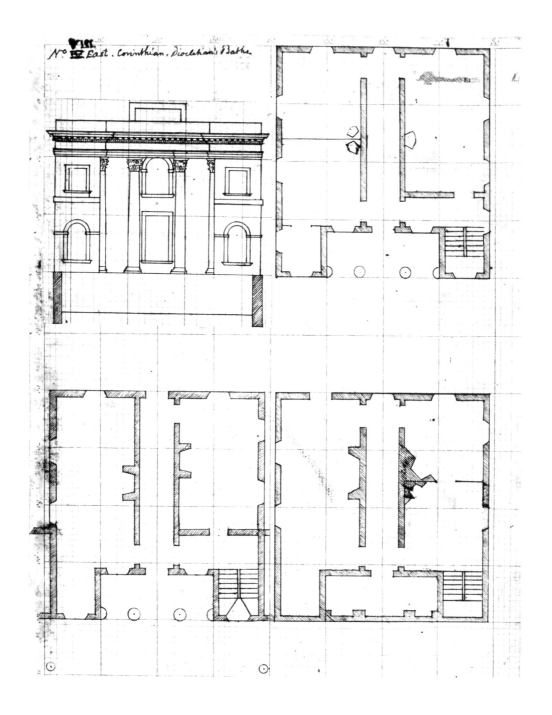

No IV East. Corinthian. Diocletian's Baths

Thomas Jefferson

Charlottesville, Virginia: Pavilion X, University of Virginia, 1819 (elevation and basement, first-floor and second-floor plans)
11 1/4" x 9 1/8", pen and brown ink on coordinate paper
Scale: 1 inch equals 10 feet
Inscribed, upper left: Pavilion No. X. East.
Specifications on reverse
Laminated in plastic
Owned by the University of Virginia
Ex coll.: Dr. Wilson Cary Nicholas Randolph, by descent

The specifications on the reverse side of the drawing state that the order is the "Doric of the Theatre of Marcellus. The columns to have no bases." It is derived from Plate II of Fréart de Chambray, where it is shown with no base but with a terminal fillet which Jefferson did not use. It was pointed out in the text that it is an unusual order and should not be used "where the eye does not have a 'free' distance" (p. 26).

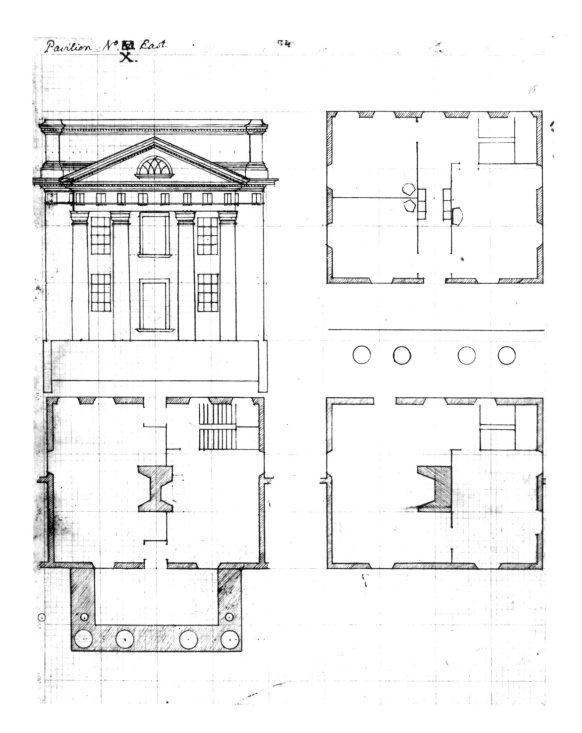

Thomas Jefferson

Charlottesville, Virginia: Pavilion X, University of Virginia, 1819 (elevation and basement, first-floor and second-floor plans)
13 1/8" x 11 1/2", pen and black ink on coordinate paper
Scale: 1 inch equals 10 feet
Inscribed (not in Jefferson's hand): Original Drawing of Mr. Jefferson's
Owned by the University of Virginia
Ex coll.: Thomas S. Ridgway, William Potts

On the reverse the following inscription appears in pencil:

An Original Drawing of Thomas Jefferson of Virginia the Author of The Declaration [of Independence] of the United States of America.
This drawing was presented to the subscriber during the winter of 1840 at the U. Va. by an aged Carpenter who was the Carpenter at the University that year stating at the time that it was a drawing of Thomas Jefferson's

> Tho. S. Ridgway
> late of the geological
> Survey of Virginia
> during the years of
> 1839 and 1840.

Presented to Master William Potts of Camden, New Jersey May 4th 1858, by the subscriber.

Although the provenance of this drawing is a little obscure, all its characteristics attest to its authenticity. Even the paper used (that designated BD in Fiske Kimball, *Thomas Jefferson, Architect* [Boston, 1916], and Frederick Doveton Nichols, *Thomas Jefferson's Architectural Drawings* [Boston, 1960]) is the same as that used for the "official" drawing for this pavilion (see preceding drawing). Is it possible to suppose from the presence of this drawing in the hands of a carpenter that the workmen used a second drawing, leaving the first, and more official, drawing in the hands of the proctor?

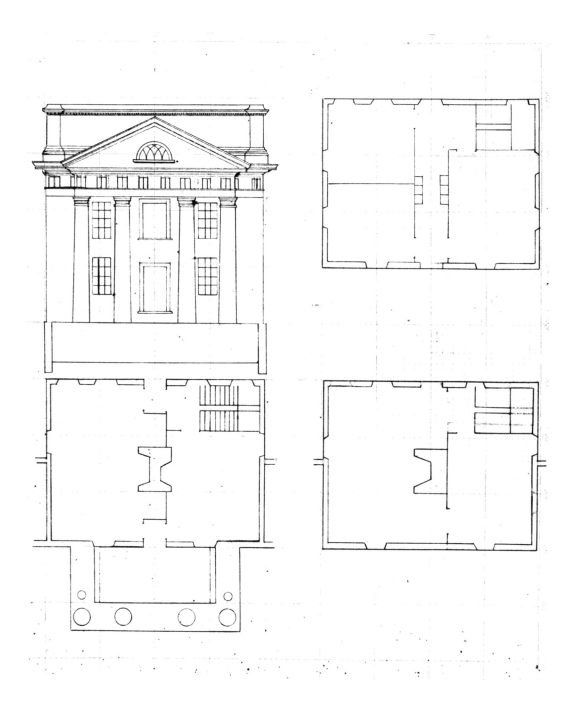

Thomas Jefferson

Charlottesville, Virginia: The Rotunda, University of Virginia, ca. 1819-21 (first-floor plan)

12 1/4" x 8 5/8", pen and brown ink, with touches of pencil, on coordinate paper

Scale: 1 inch equals 10 feet

Note: "area 1100 sq. f." appears in the left-hand room

Specifications on reverse

Laminated in plastic

Owned by the University of Virginia

Ex coll.: Dr. Wilson Cary Nicholas Randolph, by descent

This drawing was once part of a single sheet which included the succeeding drawing. The division of the plan into the three ovoid rooms may have been influenced by a conscious or unconscious memory on Jefferson's part of Plate XIII in Christian Ludwig Stieglitz, *Plans et dessins tirés de la belle architecture* (Leipzig, 1800). A similar division of a circular space appears there. Jefferson, however, had sold his copy of Stieglitz to Congress in 1815.

The dating of the Rotunda drawings cannot be fixed as exactly as that for those for the pavilions on East Lawn. They were begun at an unknown date, perhaps in 1819, and were most probably finished before March 29, 1821, when the proctor made a careful estimate of the cost of the Rotunda. They were certainly finished by April 2, 1821, when the Board of Visitors "resolved that it is expedient to proceed with the building of the Library on the plan submitted to the board."

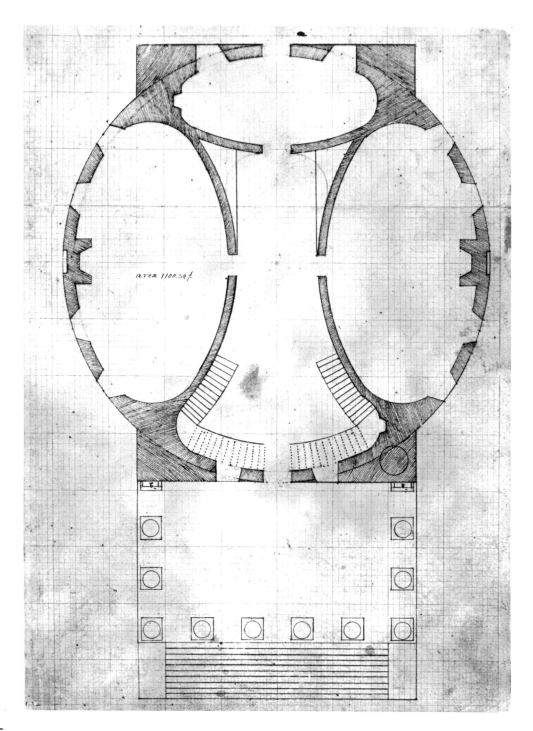

area 1100.sq.f.

Thomas Jefferson

Charlottesville, Virginia: The Rotunda, University of Virginia, 1819-21 (second, or library, floor plan)
12 1/2″ x 8 5/8″, pen and brown ink on co-ordinate paper
Scale: 1 inch equals 10 feet
Erasures show circle of inner columns moved nearer the outer walls
Specifications on reverse
Laminated in plastic
Owned by the University of Virginia
Ex coll.: Dr. Wilson Cary Nicholas Randolph, by descent

This drawing was once part of a single sheet which also contained the previous one.

The specifications on the reverse begin:

Rotunda, reduced to the proportions of the Pantheon and accommodated to the purposes of a Library for the University with rooms for drawing, music, examinations and other accessary purposes.

The diameter of the building 72. feet, being 1/2 that of the Pantheon, consequently 1/4 it's area, & 1/8 it's volume.

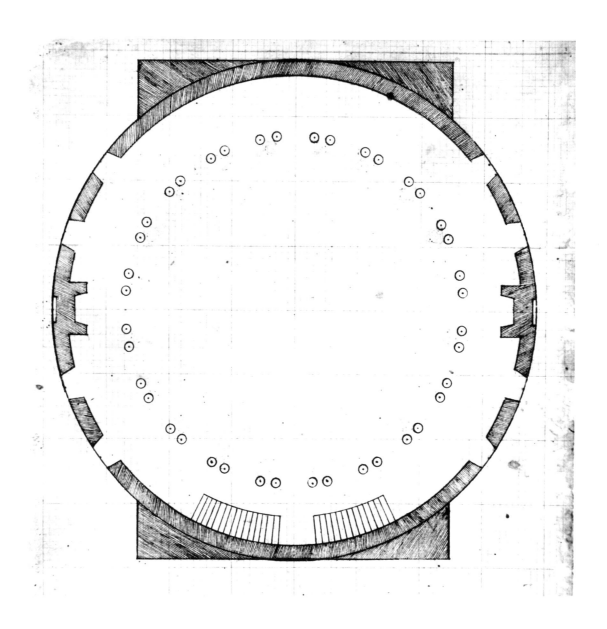

17

Thomas Jefferson

Charlottesville, Virginia: The Rotunda, University of Virginia, 1819-21 (south elevation)
8 5/8″ x 8 5/8″, pen and brown ink on coordinate paper
Scale: 1 inch equals 10 feet
Inscribed, lower left: Library
Note: left side of dome: 37° 30′
Note: right side of dome: 60°
Laminated in plastic
Owned by the University of Virginia
Ex coll.: Dr. Wilson Cary Nicholas Randolph, by descent

In his order of October 8, 1823, to Thomas Appleton at Leghorn for the capitals for the Rotunda, Jefferson finished by saying "all to be copied exactly from those of the Pantheon as represented by Palladio. B. 4. 20. pl. 60: Leoni's edition." Although he did not say so, we may assume he meant the 1721, or second, edition of Leoni's *Palladio*, since he had used it for his earlier orders for capitals for the pavilions.

The Pantheon portico has a width of seven bays, the University of Virginia Rotunda a width of only five bays. The Pantheon has a total of sixteen columns; the Rotunda only ten. The sphere enclosed in the Pantheon touches its main floor at the bottom, whereas in the Rotunda it touches the basement floor.

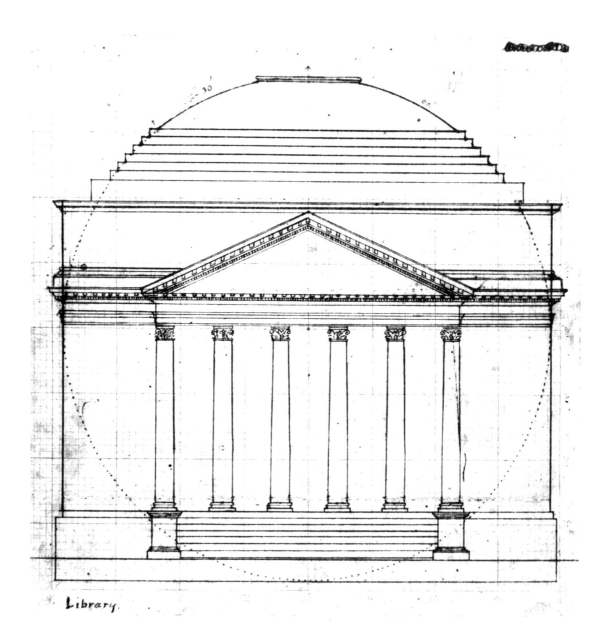

Library.

Thomas Jefferson

Charlottesville, Virginia: The Rotunda, University of Virginia, 1819-21 (section)
8 5/8" x 8 5/8", pen and brown ink on coordinate paper
Scale: 1 inch equals 10 feet
Note: The word *windows* is repeated twice in the section of the left-hand wall
Laminated in plastic
Owned by the University of Virginia
Ex coll.: Dr. Wilson Cary Nicholas Randolph, by descent

In Jefferson's letter of October 8, 1823, to Thomas Appleton at Leghorn, he asked for an estimate of the cost of the wooden capitals for the forty interior columns of the Library Room. He said they were "to be copied from Palladio B. 1. c. 18. pl. 30." The proctor's account books, however, show that these capitals were carved (in Charlottesville?) by a Philip Sturtevant.

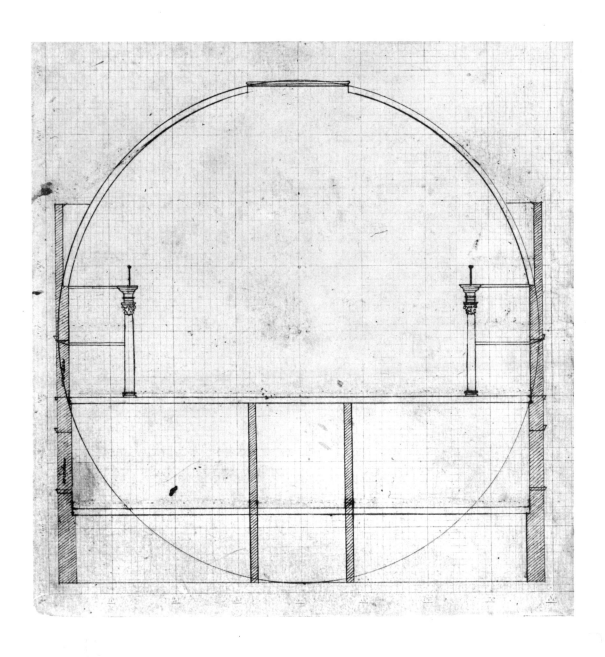

Cornelia Jefferson Randolph
1799-1871

Charlottesville, Virginia: View of the Lawn from the south, University of Virginia, ca. 1820-21
9 3/8" x 15 5/8", pen and black ink with brown, gray, and blue washes on cream paper
Mounted on linen
Owned by the University of Virginia
Ex coll.: Hartwell Cabell

The granddaughter of Jefferson, Cornelia Jefferson Randolph, was born at Monticello. Her grandfather saw that she was trained in architectural drawing, and she apparently worked under his instruction. Some of her drawings may be traced to plates in several of the books in Jefferson's library, as well as to his own drawings. The University of Virginia owns several of these and a series of her drawings in pen and ink and wash of the pavilions and hotels of the University itself.

Her elevational drawing of the Lawn omits its terrace levels. The south elevations of Pavilions IX and X show their original parapeted roofs. The original railings are in place on the students' rooms to the south of Pavilions IX and X and on the terraces above the gymnasia on either side of the Rotunda. The drawing, in spite of the mistake of its level Lawn, is probably closer to Jefferson's conception than any other respresentation of it which has survived.

23

Thomas Ustick Walter
1804-1887

Moyamensing, Pennsylvania: Philadelphia
  County Prison, Debtors, Wing, 1836 (eleva-
  tion)
13 1/4" x 19 3/4", ink and colored wash on
  paper
Scale: 1 inch equals 8 feet
Inscribed, lower center: Debtors Apartment
Inscribed, lower right: Tho. U. Walter Archt.
Dated, lower left: Dec. 26, 1836
Owned by the Royal Institute of British Archi-
  tects (presented by Walter, Dec. 17, 1838)

Thomas Ustick Walter was listed as a bricklayer
by the Philadelphia city directories as late as
1830. He became an apprentice of William
Strickland (see p. 34) and was subsequently
listed as an architect from 1835-36 on. He
became one of the nation's leading architects
and a founder and Fellow of the American Institute of Architects. His best-known work is
the dome for, and the extensions to, the Capitol
in Washington.

In Richmond, Virginia, he designed the old
First Baptist Church in the Greek Revival style
in 1841. In Norfolk, he is credited with three
works: the Old Norfolk Academy Building of
1840 in the Greek Revival style; consultation
for, and design of, the dome of the courthouse
(now the General Douglas MacArthur Memorial) of 1847-50; and the Freemason Street
Baptist Church of 1849-50 in the Gothic
Revival style. Since no drawing of any of these
buildings was located, it was thought that the
Egyptian Revival design of the Debtors' Apartment might extend knowledge of the range of
Walter's accomplishments.

DEBTORS APARTMENT

SCALE 8 FEET TO AN INCH

TNO.U.WALTER ARCH.T

John Notman
1810-1865

Philadelphia, Pennsylvania: Chapel, Laurel
   Hill Cemetery, ca. 1836-37 (elevation)
17 3/4″ x 25 1/4″, pen and ink on paper
Signed, lower left: John Not (remainder torn
   off)
Owned by The Historical Society of Penn-
   sylvania
Ex coll.: The American Institute of Architects,
   Philadelphia Chapter

John Notman, a Scot, was trained in Edinburgh.
He was in this country by 1834 and met the
chairman of the Laurel Hill Cemetry Association when he was working in Burlington, N. J.
The cemetery, laid out in 1836, was in the
picturesque style and became so admired that it
was necessary to close it to the public.

Notman was called to Richmond about 1848
to give "a more complete and precise plan
than that which had been submitted by Mr.
Pratt," who had been the first to be employed on
the design for Hollywood Cemetery. Notman
laid out another picturesque cemetery, one
which has retained much of its original character. He also provided a plan for Capitol
Square, again in the pitcuresque manner.

The drawing for the Laurel Hill Chapel,
though in a somewhat damaged condition,
captures the picturesque spirit of the cemetery's
design in its adaption of the Gothic. It was
torn down, unfortunately, because of the cost
of maintenance.

The drawing for it is part of the American
Institute of Architects, Philadelphia Chapter,
Papers, 1845-1940, a collection of eighteen
volumes and 1000 drawings and blueprints. Included in this large group there are 68 original
drawings by Notman.

Claudius Crozet
1789-1864
(Drawing by Q. H. Brown)

Middle Island Creek: A covered bridge, 1840
(plan, elevation, section, and details)
21 1/2" x 33", pen and black and red ink with
tan and gray washes on tan paper
Scale: 1 inch equals 8 feet
Inscribed, upper left: Plan of a Bridge over
Middle Island Creek | on the North Western
Turnpike
Signed, center right: This bridge was built | in
November 1838 | C. Crozet | Engr.
Signed, lower right: Drawn by Q. H. Brown |
March 1840
Owned by the Virginia State Library

The rarity of a drawing for a covered bridge, a
type of bridge which is rapidly disappearing,
makes this one doubly interesting. Not only is the
quality of its draughtsmanship extremely high,
but its structural information is far more sophis-
ticated than one would have supposed, since
these bridges are now considered to be almost
folk survivals.

It is not known why Q. H. Brown, about
whom the records are silent, drew the bridge two
years after it had been built. It may have been
an apprentice drawing made under the direction
of Crozet.

Crozet was born at Villefranche-sur-Saône,
France, in 1789. He was educated at the École
Polytechnique in Paris, but in the face of
political disturbances, he fled to the United
States in 1816. Here he taught at West Point
and then became the Surveyor of Public Works
for Virginia during three periods—1823 to 1831,
1837 to 1842, and 1848 to 1858. He always
retained an interest in education and assisted
in founding the Virginia Military Institute and
determining the character of its first courses.

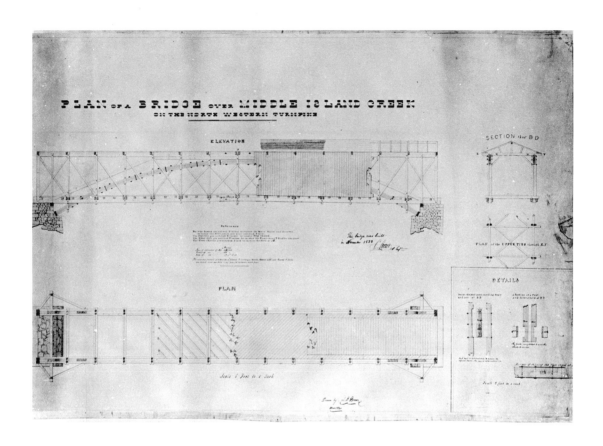

PLAN of a BRIDGE over MIDDLE ISLAND CREEK
ON THE NORTH WESTERN TURNPIKE

ELEVATION

PLAN

SECTION thro' B D

PLAN of the UPPER TIER through E F

DETAILS

G. S. Ford
active 1840 (?)

Charlottesville, Virginia: Lantern of Rotunda,
   University of Virginia, ca. 1840 (plan and
   elevation)
24 11/16″ x 22 7/16″, pen and black ink and
   gray blue wash on detail paper
Scale: 3/4 inch equals 1 foot
Inscribed, center: Plan for Rotunda Lantern
Signed, lower right: G. S. Ford
Owned by the University of Virginia

The drawing is dimensioned, and the scale is
given. Its surface is a little damaged by rubbing,
and the sheet of paper has split at the center
fold, but fortunately at a point which does not
intersect either the elevation or the plan.

The problem of the appearance and disap-
pearance of the cupolas which have been added
to the Rotunda dome at the University of Virginia is not solved as yet. One was added after
July 7, 1840, when the Board of Visitors resolved
"that the skylight of the Rotunda be altered
agreeably to a plan . . . submitted by Genl.
Cocke." This one was removed sometime after
1860 at the request of Alexander Galt, who felt
that its light would be unflattering to his statue
of Jefferson, which was to stand under it. A
second lantern was built sometime before the
1895 fire in the Rotunda. Its date is uncertain,
as is the date of its removal (before the fire?),
and the available visual evidence is inconclusive.

There is a photograph of ca. 1870 which
shows a cupola which is clearly not the one in
this drawing. Is this one, then, the drawing submitted by General John Hartwell Cocke to the
Board of Visitors in 1840?

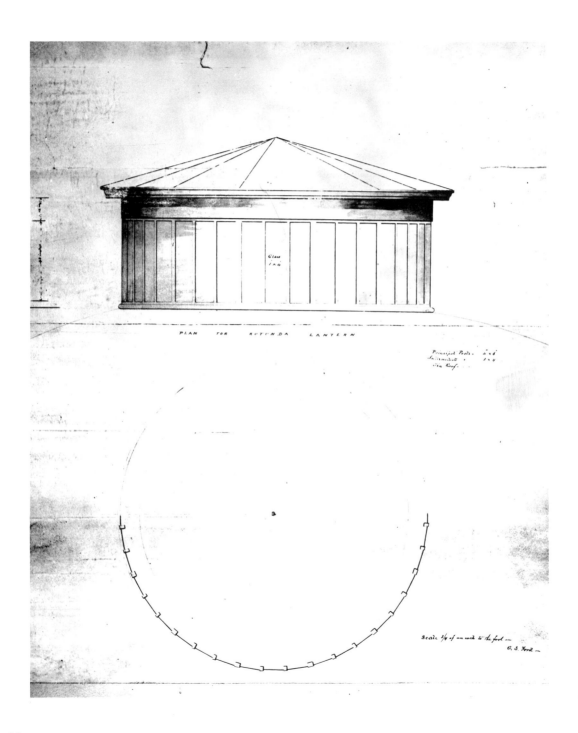

PLAN FOR ROTUNDA LANTERN

Glass
1 x 4

Principal Posts   6 x 6
Intermediate   1 x 4
Tin Roof.

Scale 1/4 of an inch to the foot
C. S. Ford

31

Oswald J. Heinrich
active 1846-1866

Germany: A student drawing (?) for a pavilion,
    1846 (plan and elevation)
16 1/2″ x 10 5/8″, pen and black ink and water
    color on cream paper
Inscribed, upper center: Entwurf eines Tagd-
    schlösschens
Signed and dated, lower right: O. Heinrich |
    $\dfrac{22 \quad 46}{I}$
Owned by the Valentine Museum
Ex coll.: O. X. Heinrich

This drawing for a pavilion in the forest (a little
day-castle) was executed before Heinrich left
Germany after the Revolution of 1848. He was
working in Augusta, Georgia, in 1852, and sometime after that date he moved to Virginia. In
Richmond he not only practiced architecture
(see p. 102) but made renderings for other
architects (see p. 80) and taught perspective.

A surviving receipt for July 29, 1859, shows
that he charged $35.00 a session for these lessons.
His notes on perspective survive. An undated
letter of correction to Edward V. Valentine be-
gins: "You will see on the Drawing that you
have established wrong the first vanishing point"
—a common error in the study of the subject.

During the Civil War, Heinrich acted as a
mine engineer for the Confederacy. It is known
that he reestablished himself in Richmond after
the war, but further records are obscure.

Entwurf eines Jagdschlößchens.

Aufriß.

Grundriß.

William Strickland
1788-1854

Cismont, Virginia: Grace Church, 1847 (plan and elevation)

15 11/16″ x 12 3/4″, pen and black ink, gray and pale yellow washes on a double sheet of lined foolscap

Scale: 1 inch equals 8 feet

Signed and dated, lower right: W. Strickland, Archt. | Nashville, 19th April | 47.

Owned by the University of Virginia

Ex coll.: Alfred Landon Rives, Miss Landon Rives, Miss Roberta Wellford

Born in New Jersey, the son of a carpenter, William Strickland was taken to Philadelphia in 1790. In 1803 he was apprenticed to the distinguished architect Benjamin Henry Latrobe. After a short time in New York, Strickland returned to Philadelphia in 1808 as a brilliant young architect, rapidly achieving national fame. He received the commission for the Tennessee State Capitol in Nashville, where he died in 1854.

The drawings (pp. 35, 37, 39) for Grace Church, Cismont, were executed at Nashville while Strickland was there working on the Capitol. They have recently been found in the papers of Alfred Landon Rives (see p. 62), whose home, Castle Hill, was near the church. Since Rives would have been only 17 in 1847, the drawings were probably preserved by his father. Grace Church was burned out at the end of the nineteenth century, but its exterior is still very much as Strickland designed it.

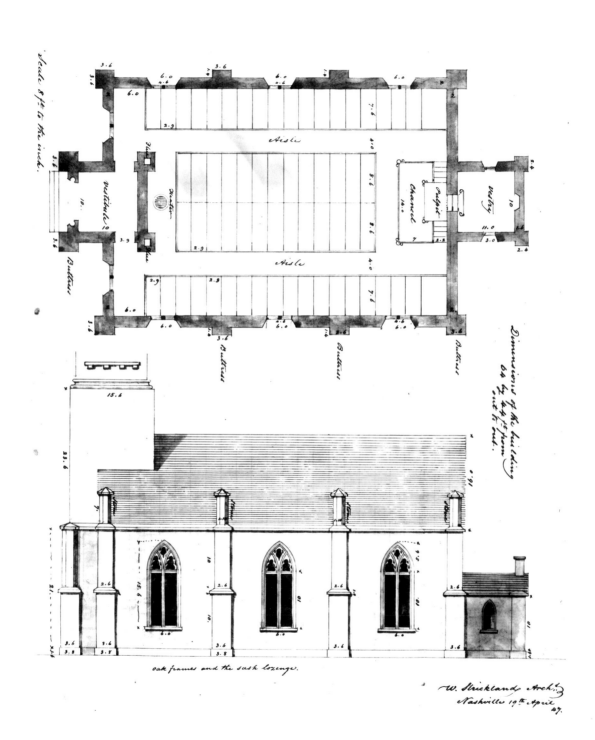

scale 8 f to the inch.

Aisle

Aisle

Chancel

Pulpit

Vestry

Dimensions of the building
64 by 42 ft from
out to out

oak frames and the sash lozenge.

W. Strickland Arch.t
Nashville 19th April
47.

William Strickland

Cismont, Virginia: Grace Church, 1847 (partial plan and half-section)

26 3/8″ x 19 5/8″, pen and black and scarlet ink on tracing paper

Scale: 1 inch equals 4 feet

Signed, lower right: W. Strickland Archt. (The signature also appears at center right)

Note, to left of the plan of the tower: Upon a level with the roof of the Portal the walls of the Tower to be reduced to 2. ft. in thickness according with the red dotted lines.

Note, to left of the portal: The Portal is to be roofed over behind the Pedimental tracery in front—14 ft. above the sill of the door of entrance.

Owned by the University of Virginia

Ex coll.: Alfred Landon Rives, Miss Landon Rives, Miss Roberta Wellford

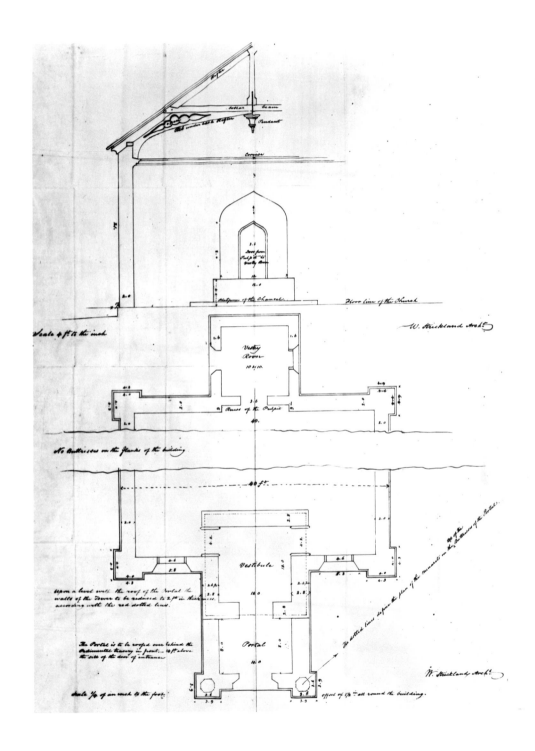

W. Strickland Arch.

Scale 4 ft. to the inch

Floor Line of the Church.

Platform of the Chancel.

Vestry
Room
10 by 10.

Recess of the Pulpit

No Buttresses on the flanks of the building

40 ft.

Vestibule

upon a level with the roof of the Portal the
walls of the Tower to be reduced to 2 ft. in thickness.
according with the red dotted lines.

The Portal is to be roofed over behind the
Ornamental Tracery in front — 16 ft. above
the sills of the door of entrance

Portal

scale ⅜ of an inch to the foot.

offset of 1½ in. all round the building.

W. Strickland Arch.

37

William Strickland

Cismont, Virginia: Grace Church, 1847 (elevation)

26 3/8″ x 19 3/4″, pen and black ink on tracing paper

Scale: 1 inch equals 4 feet

Signed, lower right: W. Strickland Archt.

Owned by the University of Virginia

Ex coll.: Alfred Landon Rives, Miss Landon Rives, Miss Roberta Wellford

Scale 4 ft. to the inch.

W. Strickland Arch.

39

"Angelo"
dates unknown

Richmond, Virginia: Competition drawing for
the Washington Monument, Capitol Square,
1849 (elevation)
25 5/8" x 16 1/4", pen and black ink on white
paper
Laminated in plastic
Owned by the Virginia State Library

"Angelo" (a pseudonym enclosed within quota-
tion marks on the printed "Description and Estimate of this Design" which accompanied it) said
that the monument "is to be of the Corinthian
order, 84 feet high and 42 at the base. To have
4 equal sides in the centre, to be a colossal statue
of Washington as first President of the United
States, to have granite plinth and 4 pillars with
marble pilasters and capitals, entablature, urns
and cupola, with iron railing . . . through one
of said pillars, to be a stair case to the reception
room."

If one may speak of a folk drawing for architecture, this is certainly a superb example. Or,
since Angelo's use of English is also over-
simplified, could the drawing be intended for a
joke?

Joseph A. Beals
active 1849

Richmond, Virginia: Drawing for the competition for the Washington Monument, Capitol Square, 1849 (plan and various details)
13 1/4" x 31 1/2", pen and black ink with wash on cream paper
Scale: 1 inch equals 1 foot [for details on right?]
Inscribed, lower center: From J. A. Beals, No. 291 Pearl St. N. Y.
Laminated in plastic
Owned by the Virginia State Library

With a letter of transmittal for a first drawing (a general scheme) Beals said that "this monument would have a more imposing effect made of your best White Marble. By my calculations and Estimates for Quarrying, working and Superintending will come within the prescribed Sum of One Hundred Thousand Dollars. Early in the following week the working plan will be transmitted, (from an accident to one of my fingers of the Right hand the plan is not as clean and as handsomely wrought up as I should wish)."

Six days later on December 5, 1849, the drawing exhibited was submitted. Beals said in the letter accompanying it that "if the general plan meets with approbation and parts that may be improved are suggested, I will take pleasure in altering them, which I should be better able to do so in a few weeks as I now suffer from my hand."

No further information about Beals has been found.

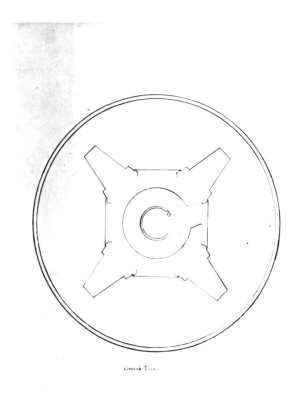

Ground Plan.

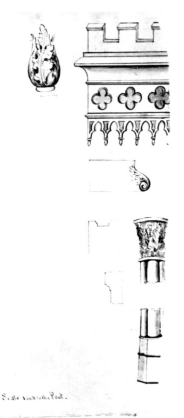

James Renwick, Jr.
1818-1895

Richmond, Virginia: Competition drawing for
    the Washington Monument, Capitol Square,
    1849 (side elevation)
29 1/4" x 22 1/4", pen and black ink
Inscribed, lower center: ... tion of Side No. 2
Laminated in plastic
Owned by the Virginia State Library

This mutilated drawing shows the side elevation of what was to have been, to judge from
the fragments of a plan extant on another sheet
in the Virginia State Library, a kind of trium-
phal arch clothed in the romantic forms of
mediaevalism.

Renwick, the son of an engineer, was educated
at Columbia College. He worked as an engineer
first on the Erie Railroad and secondly on the
district reservoir of the Croton Aqueduct at
5th Avenue and 42d Street in New York City.
By 1843 his energies were devoted to architecture, and his practice became one of the more
important ones in the country. He is noted for
his design of the original building for the Smithsonian Institution (1846-55) and of St. Patrick's
Cathedral in New York. With the introduction
of several partners his firm because known
variously as Renwick and [Joseph] Sands; Renwick and [James] Aspinwall; and Renwick,
Aspinwall, and [William W., a nephew] Renwick.

In Virginia one of his executed commissions
was that for the courthouse in Fredericksburg,
1851-52.

...TION OF SIDE N°2

45

Edward B. White
1806-1882

Richmond, Virginia: Competition drawing for the Washington Monument, Capitol Square, 1849 (elevation)

18 1/4" x 24 1/4" (sheet size) [14 5/8" x 9 7/8", drawing size], pencil and water color on white paper

Inscribed, lower center: Virginia Washington Monument. | Designed and drawn by | Edward B. White, Architect: Charleston, South Carolina. | Novr. AD. 1849

Inscribed at side with explanation of design

Laminated in plastic

Owned by the Virginia State Library

In a letter dated November 16, 1849, White said that he had "viewed the call which has been made by the Commissioners, as one which should be heard by every Son of the Land, and which should excite to action in so noble a cause, all on whom Providence has bestowed the talent." His design was entirely symbolic, even to the leaves of the capital, which are made up of those of corn, tobacco, and cotton. The curious column has thirteen shafts emblematic of the Federal Union, while the base of rocks represents the nation before being touched by civilization.

On December 3, 1849, he wrote again suggesting that a second design might be submitted "by *omitting* the mound of rocks, herbage, and fountains. And let this second Design consist of all which is shown above the top of mound; . . . except that all dimensions will be *increased* one *sixth;* which will make the height from the bottom of Pedestal to the head of the Eagle 203 feet." He added, "Both my Designs I consider in themselves complete; but, I think the first has the advantage in being more compre-

hensive, and conveying a fuller train of ideas and of thought."

Edward Brickell White was one of the better known mid-nineteenth-century architects of Charleston, South Carolina, where he was responsible for several of the more important churches and for the wings added to the old Citadel. After being educated at West Point, he was first assigned to plan a fort, but he later turned to architecture. The Civil War interrupted his career, which he found difficult to resume after the establishment of peace. He was remembered during the days of the war as a "small and rather pompous officer in very large boots, who was known to the rank and file as 'Puss in Boots.' As he rode a very large horse, the sentries never lost an opportunity to require the Colonel to dismount and advance on foot to be recognized, causing him great inconvenience both in descending from and regaining his equestrian eminence" (Beatrice St. Julien Ravenal, *Architects of Charleston* [Charleston, S. C., 1945], p. 200).

Edward B. White

Richmond, Virginia: Competition drawing for
the Washington Monument, Capitol Square,
1849 (plan and section)
23 3/4″ x 18 3/8″, pen and black ink on white
paper
Scale: 1 inch equals 18 feet
Inscribed, lower center: Virginia Monument |
Designed and drawn by Edward B. White,
Architect. Charleston South Carolina. | No-
vember, AD. 1849
Owned by the Virginia State Library

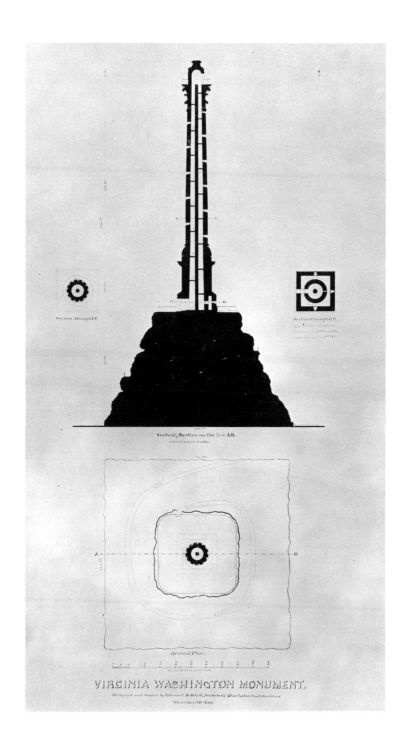

Section through EF.

Section through CD.

Vertical Section on the line AB.

Ground Plan.

VIRGINIA WASHINGTON MONUMENT.

Designed and drawn by Edward B. White, Architect, Charleston South Carolina.

49

Architect unknown

Richmond, Virginia: Competition drawing for the Washington Monument, Capitol Square, 1849 (perspective and plan)

17 1/2″ x 11″, pen and black ink and gray wash on paper

Inscribed, at bottom: 150 feet high. There are 6 faces presenting four columns at once & from the fact of the ground being in form Hexagonal there are always perspective views of two other faces.

Laminated in plastic

Owned by the Virginia State Library

This most interesting drawing has no identification, but its unusual concept seems to place its author somewhere between a trained and an untrained practitioner.

150 feet high. This will have prismatic tower shaft... from the first... ground story in form... regular time... perspective... view of the faces

Architect unknown

Richmond, Virginia: Competition drawing for
the Washington Monument, Capitol Square,
1849 (elevation)
11″ x 18″, pen and ink and wash on tan paper
Inscribed, at top: Roof (interior) Arches—In
the centre of the roof above is to be the arms
of the State of Virginia.
Inscribed, to left: The ground floor is a square
of four equal sides. Each face, like the drawing. The base to have marble panels. Alto
Relievo—subjects to be the Great Battles
of Washington. The panel next to be in
Basso Relievo. Subjects from the great events
of Washington's life & the Independence of
the U. S. [The] small panels next are for em-
blems. . . . in the Frieze the History . . .
Columbus up to the . . . Parapet panel . . .
for Inscription.
Laminated in plastic
Owned by the Virginia State Library

This mutilated and unidentified, but very able,
drawing is an excellent example of the use of
symbolism as an integral part of structures in
the mid-nineteenth century.

Thomas Crawford
1814-1857

Richmond, Virginia: Working drawing for base
    of the Washington Monument, Capitol
    Square, 1850 (plan)
26 1/2" x 29 3/4", pen and black ink on linen
Scale: 1 inch equals 4 feet
Inscribed, lower left: Duplicate No. 2
Inscribed, lower center: Ground Plan. | Scale
    of 20 Feet | Virginia Washington Monument
Signed and dated, lower right: Thos Crawford |
    May 1850
Owned by the Virginia State Library

Authorities differ on the date and place of
Thomas Crawford's birth, which are given
variously as 1813 in Ireland and 1814 in New
York City. He trained with Frazee and Launitz
in this country. In 1835 he went to Rome to
study with Thorwaldsen. There he made a
reputation, and there he spent most of the remainder of his life. His best known work is the
Armed Freedom which crowns the Capitol dome
in Washington.

When Crawford won the competition for the
Washington Monument in Richmond, he wrote
his wife on February 2, 1850, "I have beat them
all, and the monument is mine! . . . My position in art is now defined. " (Robert L. Gale,
"Thomas Crawford, Dear Lou, and the Horse,"
Virginia Magazine of History and Biography,
LXVIII [1960], 175). He did not live to complete the monument, for which some of the
figures were executed by Randolph Rogers.

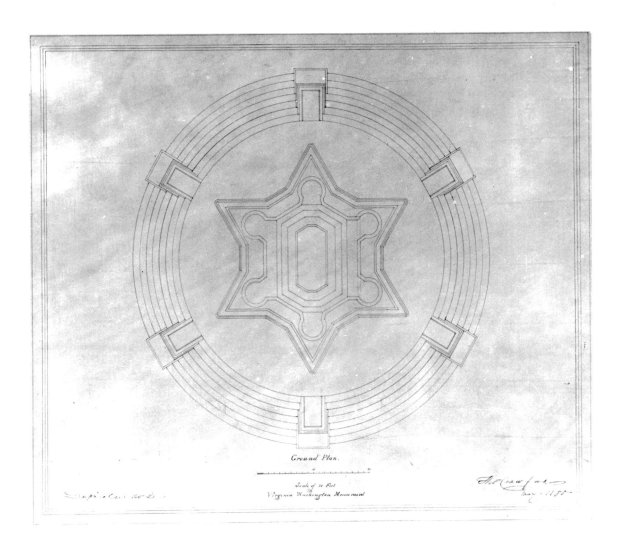

Ground Plan.

Scale of 20 Feet

Virginia Washington Monument

Tho? Crawford
May . 1850

55

Thomas Crawford

Richmond, Virginia: Working drawing for the Washington Monument, Capitol Square, 1850 (side elevation)

27" x 29 3/4", pen and black and scarlet ink on linen

Scale: 1 inch equals 4 feet

Inscribed, lower left: Virginia Washington Monument

Inscribed, lower center: Side Elevation | Scale of 20 Feet | Wreaths to be of Bronze

Inscribed, lower right: Red lines indicate positions and height | of Bronze Statuary | Duplicate of No. 5

Signed and dated, lower left: Thos. Crawford/ May 1850

Owned by the Virginia State Library

There are a number of these working drawings at the Virginia State Library, of which only three have been selected for inclusion in this exhibition.

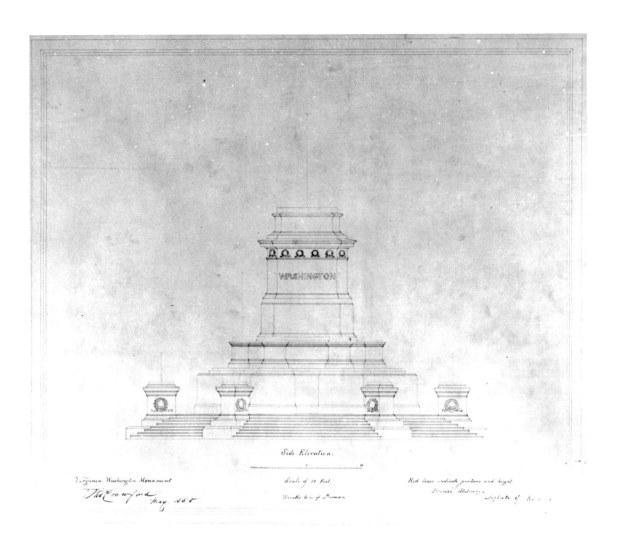

Side Elevation.

Virginia Washington Monument   Scale of 20 Feet   Red lines indicate positions and height

Th.ᵒ Crawford   Bronze Statuary.
              May 1855   Wrought to in of Bronze

Thomas Crawford

Richmond, Virginia: Working drawing for the Washington Monument, Capitol Square, 1850 (iron stair)

27″ x 15 1/4″, pen and black ink on linen

Scale: 2 inches equal 1 foot

Inscribed, upper left: Duplicate of | No. 16

Inscribed, center: Elevation of Iron Stair

Inscribed, lower left: Virginia | Washington Monument

Inscribed, lower center: Plan of Iron Stair, with mode of perforation | required for each tread, for the passage of Light | From window in platform of Equestrian Statue.

Signed and dated, lower left: Thos Crawford | May 1850

Owned by the Virginia State Library

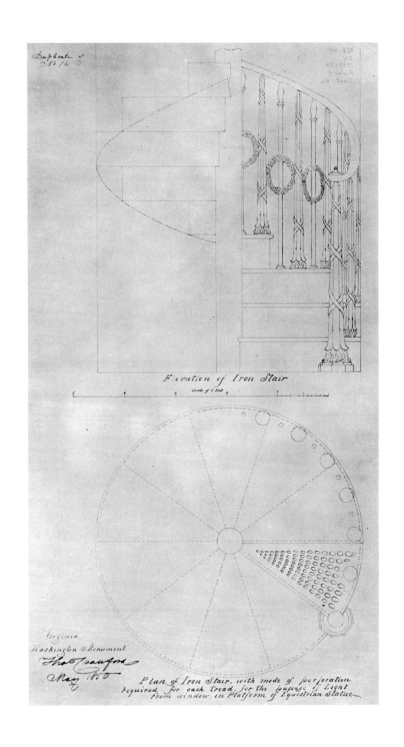

Elevation of Iron Stair

Plan of Iron Stair, with mode of perforation
required for each tread, for the passage of Light
from window in Platform of Equestrian Statue.

Virginia
Washington Monument
Thos Crawford
May 1850

Oswald J. Heinrich
active 1846-1866

Augusta, Georgia: A residence, 1852 (front and side elevations and basement, first-floor and second-floor plans)

18 1/4" x 26", pen and black ink and water color on white paper

Signed and dated, lower right: fec: Osw Heinrich. Ingenieur | Augusta, Ga. d. 18 Jan. 1852

Owned by the Valentine Museum

Ex coll.: O. X. Heinrich

This design for a mid-nineteenth-century house is a splendid example of the many influences which entered into the architecture of the time. Since it also demonstrates a very definite step in the development of Heinrich, it is included in the exhibition.

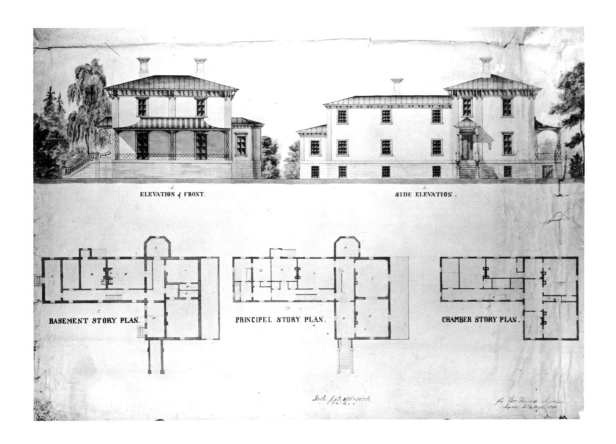

ELEVATION of FRONT.

SIDE ELEVATION.

BASEMENT STORY PLAN.

PRINCIPEL STORY PLAN.

CHAMBER STORY PLAN.

Alfred Landon Rives
1830-1903

Railway carriage, ca. 1852
14 1/2" x 21 5/8", pen and black ink on co-
   ordinate paper with notations in pencil
Inscribed, upper center: Wagon-Salon
Inscribed, upper left: Rives
Signed, lower right: Alfred L. Rives
Owned by the University of Virginia
Ex coll.: Alfred Landon Rives, Miss Landon
   Rives, Miss Roberta Wellford

Alfred Landon Rives was born in Paris, France,
on March 25, 1830. His father, William Cabell
Rives, was then the U.S. Minister to France,
and his mother was the former Judith Page
Walker, the daughter of Francis Walker of
Castle Hill, Virginia. Alfred Rives was educated at the University of Virginia and the Virginia Military Institute; when his father was for
the second time appointed U.S. Minister to
France (1849-53), he completed his training at
the École Imperiale des Ponts et Chaussées in
Paris.

When he returned to this country, he was the
assistant engineer for the completion of the
Capitol in Washington; an engineer on the
Washington aqueduct; and in charge of the
U.S. survey for improving the Potomac. When
the Civil War broke out, he returned to Virginia
and served as a colonel of engineers in the Con-
federate army.

After the war he worked with many railroads
—the Chesapeake and Ohio, the South and
North Alabama, the Mobile and Ohio, the Richmond and Danville, and the Panama Railroad.
He was also the chief engineer for the Cape Cod
Canal and was even offered the post of chief
of the civil engineering works in Egypt, which
he refused.

Richmond was his base for these activities.

That he was also considered an architect is
proved by entries in the faculty minutes and
other reports of the College of William and
Mary. He was called in to work on the Wren
Building after its third fire—the first was in
1705, the second in 1859, and the third in
1862—and completed its fourth version.

The minutes state that

the rebuilding of the College having been ordered
by the Board of Visitors and Governors . . .
it was resolved that this sum, ten thousand dollars, be appropriated. . . . Colonel Alfred L.
Rives of Richmond having been appointed
Architect by the Building Committee, was
recognized as such (October 11, 1867, Faculty
Minutes, William and Mary).

The next year the building was almost finished, and it is good to learn that Rives had been
paid.

Early in July last the Building Committee
appointed by you at your Convocation of July
3, 1867, met, organized and elected Col. Alfred
L. Rives Architect and took other necessary steps
for commencing to rebuild the main college
edifice. In August a general plan was presented
and approved and contracts for material ordered. The plan and elevation accompany this re-
port. . . . The principal part is now done. . . .

Sept.-Dec.—Services of Architect $232.00. To
finish and furnish the building will require
$5000 more. (July 3, 1868, Report of the Build-
ing Committee, College of William and Mary
to the Board of Visitors)

The drawing of the railway carriage is, of
course, a student drawing. The elevation is
dimensioned. Notice especially the color notes
on the body of the carriage. It is to be largely
black with blue panels, with a brilliant coat of
arms on the door in red, green, gold, and light
gray.

WAGON - SALON.

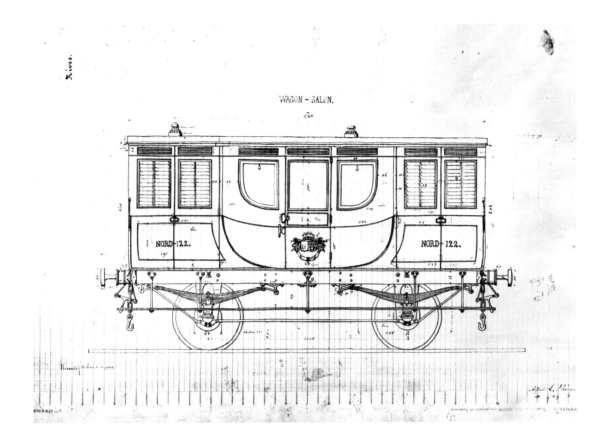

NORD - 122.

NORD - 122.

Alfred Landon Rives

A masonry bridge, 1852-53 (elevation and section)

25 1/2" x 39", pen and black and blue ink on cream paper, touched with yellow, brown, blue, red, lavender, and gray washes

Inscribed, upper center: Projet de Pont

Stamped, upper left: 2e Classe | 1er Concours de Construction

Impressed: 1852-1853/EIPC

Signed, upper right: Rives

Owned by the University of Virginia

Ex coll.: Alfred Landon Rives, Miss Landon Rives, Miss Roberta Wellford

This student drawing of 1852-53 shows both a half elevation and a half section of the first arch of a masonry bridge, including the framework for the centering on which the arch could be built. The elevation is beautifully rendered with washes, and the drawing is of considerable structural as well as architectural interest.

The initials EIPC in the impressed stamp stand for École Imperiale des Ponts et Chaussées.

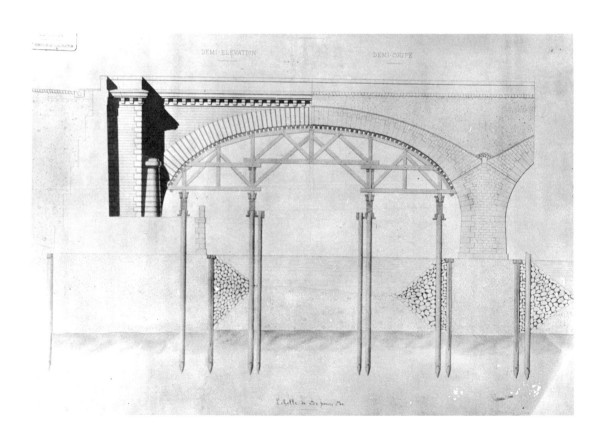

Alfred Landon Rives

Design for a pier, ca. 1854 (front and side elevations, plan, and section)
27 7/16″ x 43 3/8″, pen and black, red, and blue ink with pink and blue washes on white paper mounted on linen
Inscribed, at upper left: Chemin de Fer | de | Marseilles à Avignon
Inscribed, at upper center: Piles
Inscribed, at upper right: Viaduc du Rhone
Signed, lower right: Alfred L. Rives
Owned by the University of Virginia
Ex coll.: Alfred Landon Rives, Miss Landon Rives, Miss Roberta Wellford

The two elevations and two plans are partially dimensioned. It is not clear whether this drawing is a student design or whether it is a study of the actual bridge used by the Marseilles-Avignon railway. It is an expressive drawing and full of information of the continuing use of masonry within the age of iron.

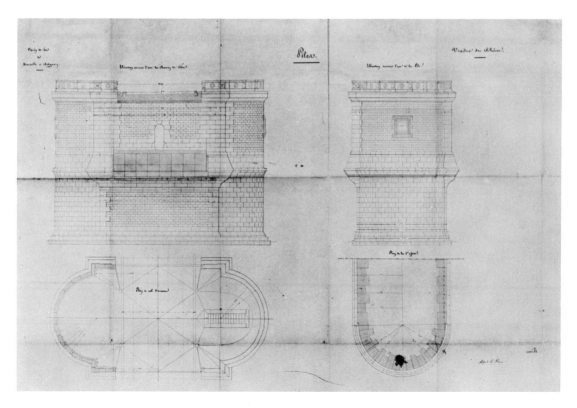

Alfred Landon Rives

Design for a cast-iron bridge, ca. 1854 (elevation)

23 3/4" x 73 1/2", pen and black and red ink on white paper mounted on linen

Inscribed, upper center: Viaduc du Rhone | Arc de Rive

Signed, lower right: Alfred L. Rives

Owned by the University of Virginia

Ex coll.: Alfred Landon Rives, Miss Landon Rives, Miss Roberta Wellford

This elevation of a cast-iron span for a bridge is a part of the study of the same bridge as the preceding drawing. It shows considerable elegance in the use of the iron, both in the structure of the arch itself and in the decorative features of the rail.

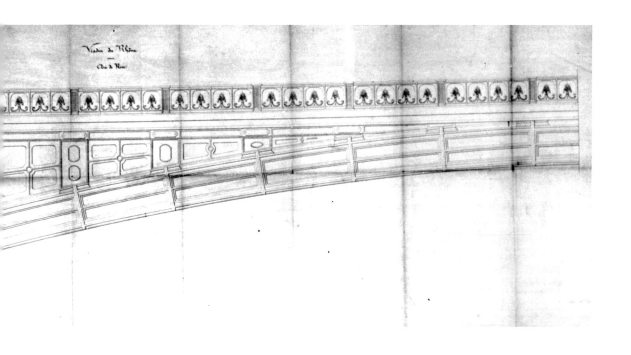

Viaduc du Rhône

Vue de Face

Alfred Landon Rives

Study for a railroad station, 1854 (end elevation)
12" x 28", pencil and pen and red ink touched
   with gray and pink washes on cream tracing
   paper
Inscribed, on reverse: Donné à Strasbourg par
   un conducteur des Ponts et Chaussées | 21
   Juillet 1854. | Alfred L. Rives.
Owned by the University of Virginia
Ex coll.: Alfred Landon Rives, Miss Landon
   Rives, Miss Roberta Wellford

The Victorian habit of using new structural
methods in juxtaposition with building forms of
the past is seen very clearly in this study. The
train sheds of cast iron with their vented skylights
represent the new techniques of the mid-nineteenth century. The pavilions on either side of
the tracks, however, look back nostalgically to
Italy's past for their architectural form.

There is a slight question of authorship for
this drawing. If *donné* means given as a gift,
then clearly the drawing is not by Rives. If,
however, it means given in the sense of assigning
an exercise or a problem to a student, then it
may be accepted as by Rives. Acceptance of the
latter meaning is strengthened by the similar
techniques seen here and in other drawings by
Rives, and it seems to be by his hand.

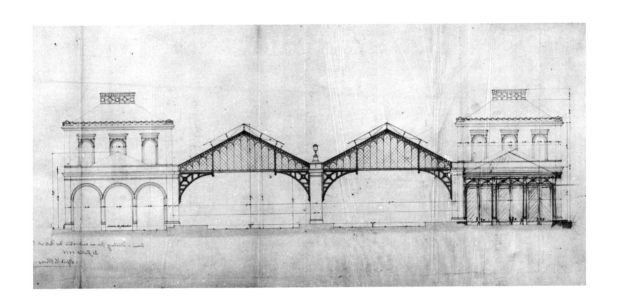

Richard Upjohn
1801-1878

Alexandria, Virginia: House of Bishop Johns, 1854 (front and side elevations)
8″ x 20″, pen and ink and wash on white paper
Scale: 1 inch equals 8 feet
Inscribed, lower center: House for Rt. Rev. Bishop Johns. | Virginia.
Signed, lower right: Richard Upjohn & Co | Trinity Building | N. Y.
Dated, lower left: April 1st, 1854. N.Y.
Owned by Avery Library, Columbia University
Ex coll.: Everard Upjohn

Richard Upjohn came to this country from England as a young man. He settled in New Bedford, Massachusetts, where he worked as a draughtsman and a teacher of drafting. By 1833 he was advertising for work on "Architectural Plans and Elevations." He soon had a wider than local reputation, and his work took him to Boston and Maine.

In Boston he met Dr. Jonathan Mayhew Wainwright, who became the rector of Trinity Church, New York, in 1837. It was through Dr. Wainwright that Upjohn was called to New York to work on a new Trinity Church, a building which was to become a monument of the Gothic Revival in America.

Upjohn became noted in church circles both for his architecture and for his pious adherence to strict principles of Christian design. It is not surprising, then, to find him designing a house for Bishop Johns as far afield as Virginia. It is thought, but not quite certain, that this house was to be built in Alexandria. The correspondence for it runs from October 19, 1853, to July 26, 1854. Bishop Johns sent a check for $200 for the design, and the house cost $5,000.

Besides this house Upjohn also designed residences for C. J. Leigh and W. B. Stanard in Richmond, 1853; Christ Church rectory, Norfolk, 1853; alterations for the chancel and furniture of Monumental Church, Richmond, 1847, and a cottage at White Sulphur Springs (then in Virginia), 1854 (?).

This drawing has lost its section but shows a typical, rather plain, mid-Victorian house. It was given to the Avery Library as a part of the Upjohn Collection by Everard Upjohn, Richard Upjohn's biographer and great-grandson.

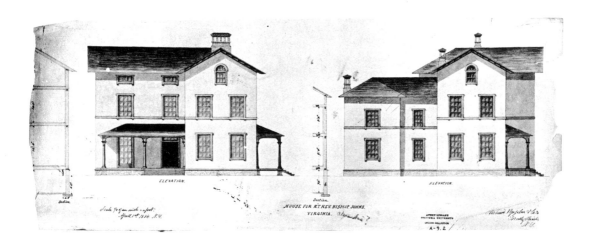

ELEVATION.

ELEVATION.

Section.

HOUSE FOR RT. REV. BISHOP JOHNS.
VIRGINIA. Alexandria?

Scale ¼ of an inch = a foot.
April 1st 1854. N.Y.

Alfred Landon Rives
1830-1903

Design for a railroad station, 1854-55 (elevation and plan)

25 3/4" x 39 5/8", pen and black and blue ink with tan, brown, blue, and gray washes on cream paper

Inscribed: Projet d'une Station | de | Chemin de Fer

Stamped, upper left: 2e Classe | Concours d'Architecture

Impressed: 1854-1855 | EIPC

Signed, upper right: Rives

Owned by the University of Virginia

Ex coll.: Alfred Landon Rives, Miss Landon Rives, Miss Roberta Wellford

The place name inscribed on the façade of this railroad station is Cobham, the post office name for Rives's Virginia home, Castle Hill. The use of metal in the cut-metal valances and cast-iron columns of the flanking covered ways shows a basic understanding of the new techniques. The plan indicates an increasing ability on the part of Rives to solve the problems of circulation for what was at that time a comparatively new building type.

The University owns a number of Rives's student drawings which are not shown in this exhibition. They are variously stamped "Concours d'Architecture" and "Concours de Construction" and date from the academic years 1851-52 through 1855-56.

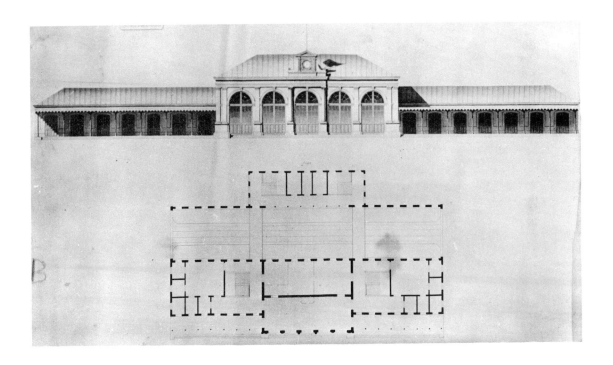

Thomas Alexander Teft
1826-1859

Richmond, Virginia: Richmond Female Institute, ca. 1855 (perspective)
15″ x 19 3/8″, pencil and water color on cream
   paper
Inscribed, lower center: Perspective View | of
   the | Richmond Female Institute | Richmond,
   Va.
Inscribed, lower right: T. A. Teft, Archt.
Owned by Brown University

Thomas Alexander Teft was a native of Rhode
Island. He went to Providence in 1844 to work
with Tallman and Bucklin. Somewhat later he
attended Brown University, graduating in 1851.
He quickly became prominent for his buildings
commissioned by various Baptist churches, including the Richmond Female Institute. Having
sailed for Europe in 1856, he died in Rome in
1859. He had, however, become a charter member of the American Institute of Architects in
1857.

   The Richmond Female Institute chartered
in 1853, was built at 10th and Marshall streets.
It became subsequently the Women's College of
Richmond, then Westhampton College of Richmond College, which, in turn, became the University of Richmond.

PERSPECTIVE VIEW
OF THE
RICHMOND FEMALE INSTITUTE
RICHMOND VA.

T. A. Tefft, Arch't

75

Norris G. Starkweather
active 1856–d. 1885

Caroline County, Virginia: Camden, 1856 (perspective)
20″ x 36″, water color on white paper
Owned by Mr. and Mrs. Richard T. Pratt

Camden, finished and furnished by 1859, is
one of the most extraordinary Victorian houses
in existence. Built as a gift for his bride by
William C. Pratt, its drawing room is still intact
with its original furnishings, and large portions
of its original heating system (the ducts), plumbing system, and lighting system are still in place
and still working. Its single loss is the upper
portion of the entrance tower, shot off during the
Civil War by gunboats passing on the Rap-
pahannock.

The architect's drawings still hang in the
house. Norris G. Starkweather practiced in both
Baltimore and Washington. He used the same
Italianate style of Camden for a house at
Hampton, Maryland, the Gothic style for the
rectory of the Church of the Redeemer, Baltimore, and various other ecclesiastical commissions in Baltimore, Washington, and George-
town, a cast-iron frame for the First Presbyterian
Church in Baltimore, and, after the Civil War,
the French style with mansard roof for several
commissions.

Norris G. Starkweather

Caroline County, Virginia: Camden, 1856
  (river and drive elevations)
20″ x 30″, pen and gray ink and water color on
  cream paper
Scale: 1 inch equals 8 feet
Inscribed, lower center: Elevations | of | Italian
  Villa | for | William C. Pratt | Camden Place
Inscribed, lower right: N. G. Starkweather |
  Architect | Baltimore & Washington
Owned by Mr. and Mrs. Richard T. Pratt

It should be noted that the tradition of using the
river as a highway was still in effect at the time
Camden was built. Thus its river front assumed
equal importance with its drive front.

Norris G. Starkweather

Caroline County, Virginia: Camden, 1856
   (side elevation)
20″ x 30″, pen and gray ink and water color
Scale: 1 inch equals 2 feet
Inscribed, lower center: Side Elevation | of |
   Italian Villa for W. C. Pratt Esqr.
Inscribed, lower right: N. G. Starkweather | Architect | Balt. & Wash.
Owned by Mr. and Mrs. Richard T. Pratt

The orangery, the central feature of this elevation, had a dirt floor at the level of the ground to receive the plants. It had, at the level of the porch, a balcony which was separated from the rest of the orangery by glazing and from which one could enter the house itself or inspect the plants.

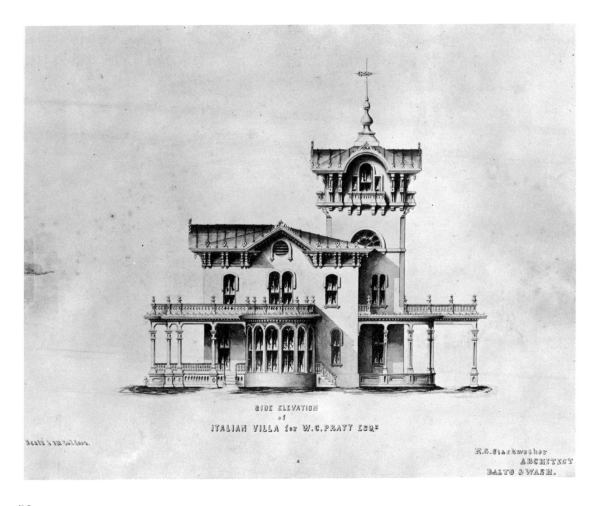

Oswald J. Heinrich
active 1846-1866

Richmond, Virginia: Monroe Tomb, Hollywood Cemetery, 1858 (perspective)
26" x 20", water color on white paper
Signed and dated: O. Heinrich, fec. | 1858
Owned by the Valentine Museum
Ex coll.: Miss Franziska Wipperman

Miss Wipperman, Heinrich's granddaughter, believed he designed Monroe's Tomb, but the
Richmond Dispatch for December 24, 1858,
stated that Governor Wise gave the commission
to Albert Lybrock (see p. 82), who prepared the
Gothic temple which the governor preferred. It
further stated that Wood and Perot of Philadelphia had contracted for casting it in iron.
Heinrich, who executed the drawing, presumably
was employed for this purpose by Lybrock.

   This remarkable monument has survived, and
several features of the view of Capitol Hill
behind it may still be discerned.

Albert Lybrock
active 1858

Richmond, Virginia: The Capitol, 1858 (front elevation)
18 1/2" x 28", pen and black ink with gray, blue, and brown wash on mounted paper
Scale: 1 inch equals 8 feet
Inscribed, upper center: State House | Richmond, Va.
Inscribed, lower center: Front. Elevation
Signed and dated, lower right: Alb. Lybrock archt & sup't. | Richmond, Va. January 1858
Owned by the Virginia State Library

This is a measured drawing of the Capitol at Richmond as it was in 1858. The front flight of steps, as designed by Jefferson and incorporated in the model by Clérisseau, had not yet been built. The principal entrances, then, were up the steps at the sides as seen here, with a minor entrance at the front through the basement of the portico. In his next drawing Lybrock proposed to return to Jefferson's original concept.

Very little is known about Lybrock except that he also worked on the U.S. Post Office and Custom House in some capacity and won the commission for the Monroe Tomb.

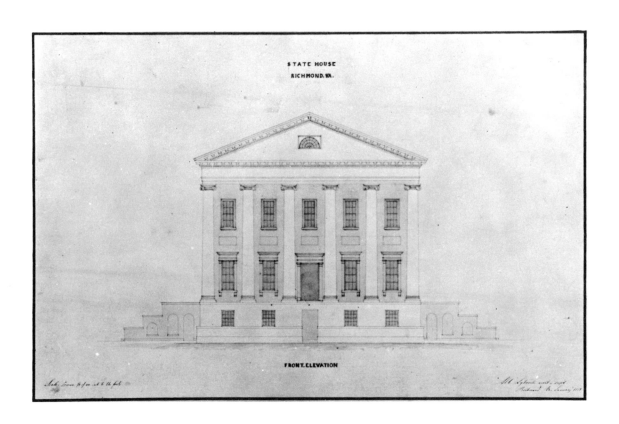

STATE HOUSE
RICHMOND. VA.

FRONT. ELEVATION

83

Albert Lybrock

Richmond, Virginia: The Capitol, 1858 (front elevation)

18 1/2″ x 21 1/4″, pen and black ink with gray, blue, and brown washes on mounted board

Scale: 1 inch equals 8 feet

Inscribed, upper center: State-House | Richmond, Virginia

Inscribed, lower center: Front Elevation. | *as proposed*

Signed and dated, lower right: Alb Lybrock, archt. & sup't | Richmond, Va. January 1858.

Owned by the Virginia State Library

In this design Lybrock returned to the concept of a flight of steps leading to the front portico of the Capitol at Richmond, but he substituted a window at the center of the first floor for the existing door. In addition, he removed the side flights of stairs and the unfortunate window in the center of the pediment, a window which had so ruined the temple effect in the early photographs of the building. Some of these changes were carried out after the Civil War.

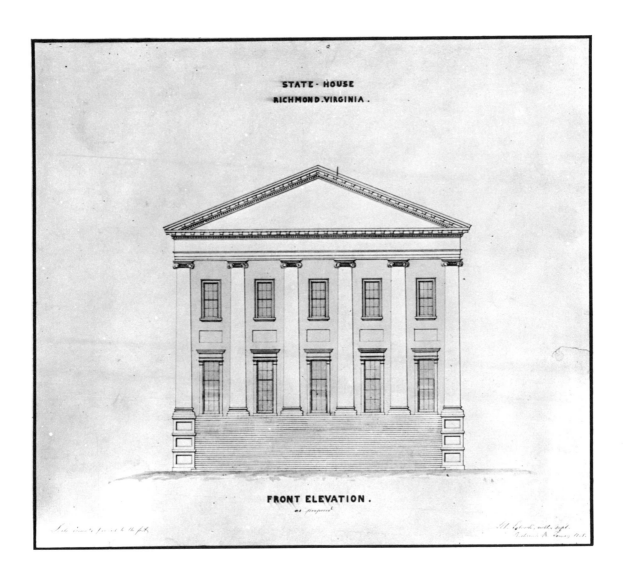

STATE · HOUSE
RICHMOND · VIRGINIA ·

FRONT ELEVATION ·
as proposed

85

Alexander Jackson Davis
1803-1892

Lexington, Virginia: Superintendent's residence,
    Virginia Military Institute, 1860 (first-floor
    plan)
11″ x 17 3/4″, pen and black ink with tan, pink,
    and yellow wash on cream paper
Scale: 1 inch equals 8 feet
Inscribed: Plan No. 2. Principal floor | Adopted
    for the executive Mansion | Va. Military In-
    stitute. Lexington, Va. | 1860
Owned by Virginia Military Institute

Alexander Jackson Davis, a native New Yorker,
began his education with the Antique School,
later the Academy of Design, in New York. He
then was apprenticed to Josiah R. Brady, architect, and studied for a short time at the old
Athenaeum in Boston in 1827. During that
same year he began work with Ithiel Town
and was made a partner in 1829. The firm of
Town and Davis became one of the best, as well
as best-known, in the country.

After Town's death in 1844, Davis continued
the office alone, executing innumerable commissions with great energy and success. He established a large architectural library in his office
and was one of the founders of the National Institute of Architects in 1836, as he was also of
the American Institute of Architects in 1857.
He became a trustee of this latter body when it
came into existence.

In Virginia he designed many buildings, not
only in Lexington where he executed the entire
group for the Virginia Military Institute, but
in Richmond, Middletown, Alexandria, Powhatan County, Albemarle County, Amelia County,
Green Springs, and Lynchburg. The commission
for Belmead, the home of Colonel Philip St.
George Cocke, probably led to Davis's work at
Virginia Military Institute, for Colonel Cocke
was a member of the board of the then young
institution.

This drawing and the succeeding elevation
show the Superintendent's house as it was built.
The residence is no longer on its original site,
for it was moved back to its present position in
order to enlarge the parade ground at a sub-
sequent date.

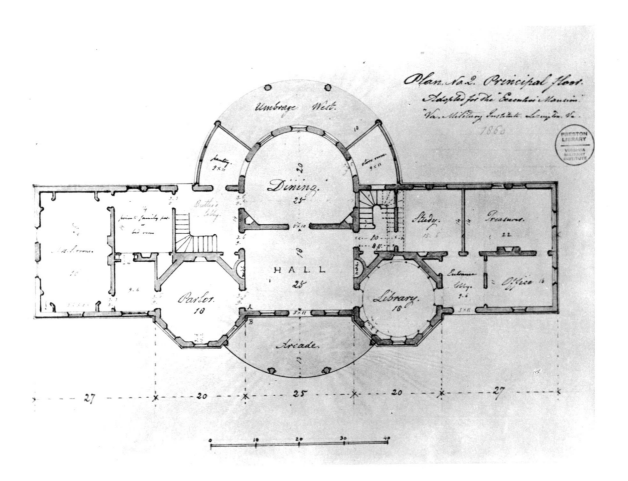

Plan No 2. Principal floor.

Adapted for the "Executive Mansion"

Va. Military Institute, Lexington Va.

1860

Umbrage West.

Dining. 25

store rooms. 9 x 11

Study. 15 8

Treasures. 22

HALL. 28

Parlor. 18

Library. 18

Office 16

Entrance Lobby. 9.6

Arcade.

Butler's Lobby.

parlor & family parlor bed rooms

27   20   25   20   27

0   10   20   30   40

Alexander Jackson Davis

Lexington, Virginia: Superintendent's residence,
    Virginia Military Institute, 1860 (elevation)
13 3/8"x 18 1/2", pen and black ink and water
    color on cream paper
Scale: 1 inch equals 8 feet
Inscribed: Executive Mansion Va. Military Inst.
    Lexington, Va. | 1860
Owned by Virginia Military Institute

Executive Mansion Va. Military Inst. Lexington Va.
1860.

89

Alexander Jackson Davis

Lexington, Virginia: Faculty residence, Virginia Military Institute, ca. 1860 (first-floor plan and elevation)

17″ x 23″, pen and black ink with black and orange wash on plan and water color on elevation on cream paper

Scale: 1 inch equals 4 feet (plan only)

Inscribed: River Front

Owned by Virginia Military Institute

This and the succeeding Davis designs were not built. They are a part of the large number of sheets related to the Virginia Military Institute which have survived. Although many of them are in various depositories, the Institute has recently purchased a group from which the five exhibited here have been chosen. They had been in the possession of the family of an anonymous collector who had obtained them from the original auction of Davis's effects.

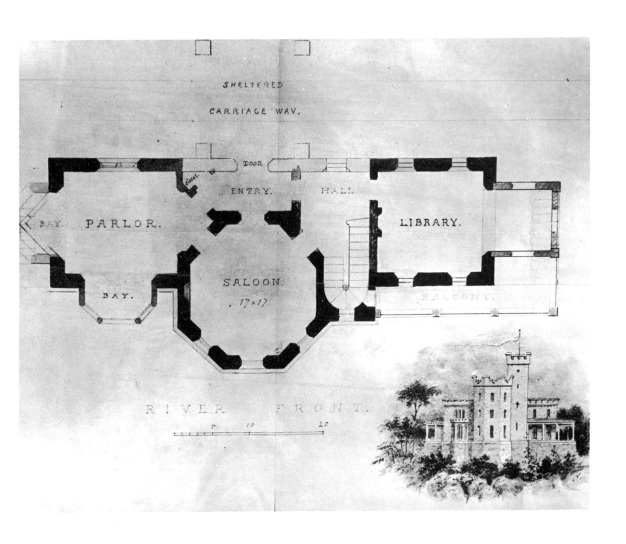

SHELTERED

CARRIAGE WAY.

DOOR

Closet.

ENTRY.   HALL

BAY.   PARLOR.

LIBRARY.

BAY.

SALOON.

. 17×17

BALCONY.

R I V E R   F R O N T.

10   20

Alexander Jackson Davis

Lexington, Virginia: Faculty residence, Virginia
    Military Institute, ca. 1860 (front elevation
    and principal floor plan)
17″ x 14″, pen and black ink with blue, pink,
    yellow, and black wash on plan and water
    color on elevation on white paper
Inscribed : Study for VMI
Owned by Virginia Military Institute

This building was not built.

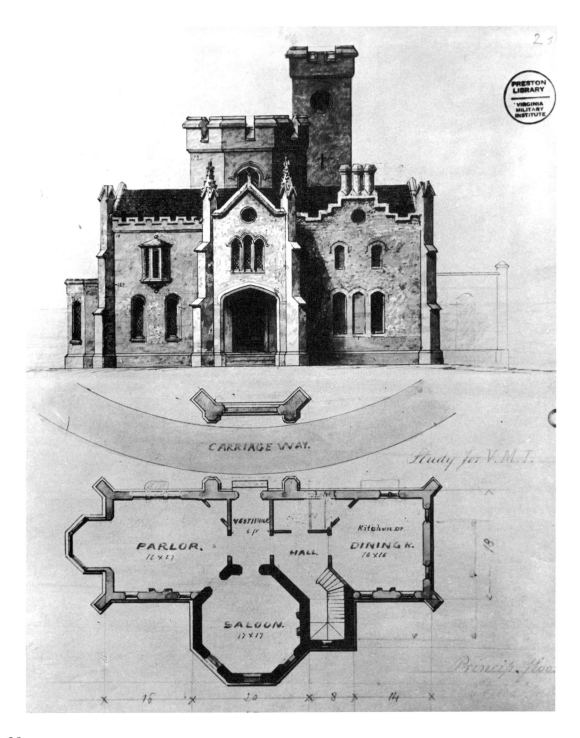

CARRIAGE WAY.

Study for V.M.I.

VESTIBULE
6 ft

Kitchen or

PARLOR.
16 x 27

HALL.

DINING R.
16 x 16

SALOON.
17 x 17

Princip. Floo.

93

Alexander Jackson Davis

Lexington, Virginia: Faculty residence, Virginia
  Military Institute, ca. 1860 (side elevation
  and second-floor plan)
17" x 13 7/8", pen and black ink with pink,
  yellow, lavender, and dark brown wash on
  plan and water color on elevation on white
  paper
Scale: 1 inch equals 8 feet
Inscribed: Upper story | VMI Study
Owned by Virginia Military Institute

This building was not built.

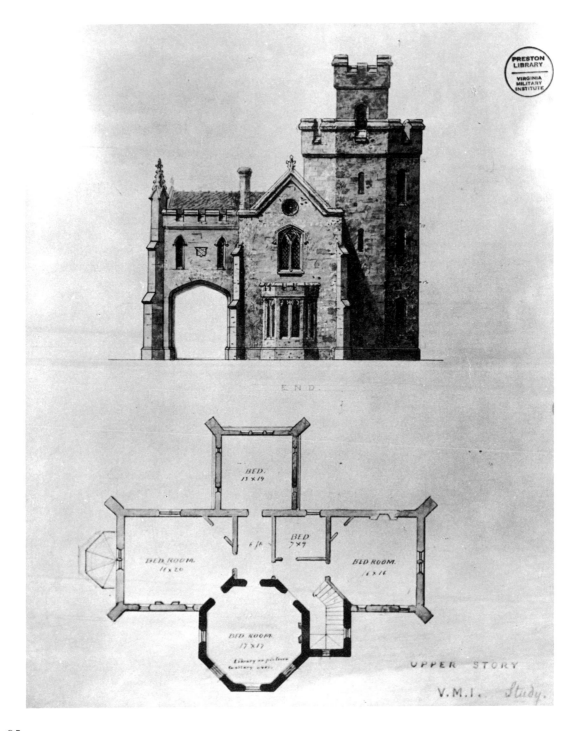

END.

BED.
13 × 14

BED ROOM.
16 × 20

BED
7 × 9

BED ROOM.
16 × 16

BED ROOM
17 × 17

Library or picture
Gallery over.

UPPER STORY

V.M.I. Study.

95

Alfred Landon Rives
1830-1903

Richmond, Virginia (?) : Design for a business
   block (1103 East Main Street ?), ca. 1865
   (elevation)
23 3/16" x 17 7/8", pen and black ink with
   washes of pink, brown, blue, and gray on
   cream paper.
Owned by the University of Virginia
Ex coll.: Alfred Landon Rives, Miss Landon
   Rives, Miss Roberta Wellford

This drawing is a rendered copy of a print (?)
or line drawing found in the Rives Collection.
Whether the print had been supplied by a cast-
iron manufacturer or not is uncertain. The date
is also uncertain, but it is known that Rives
settled in Richmond after the Civil War, and
that Richmond's great age of the iron front
began immediately after the end of that war.

The peculiar perspective of the sidewalk is the
one awkwardness which appears in the Rives
drawings. Since this drawing is not signed, it
may be by another hand, but the technique of
the washes is so similar to that on his student
drawings (see pp. 64, 65, 66-67, 69, and 73)
that the attribution seems quite probable.

97

Alfred Landon Rives

Richmond, Virginia (?) : Design for a business
   block (1103 East Main Street ?), ca. 1865
   (side elevation)
16 9/16″ x 24 1/4″, pen and black ink with
   washes of pink, blue, and gray on cream
   paper
Owned by the University of Virginia
Ex coll.: Alfred Landon Rives, Miss Landon
   Rives, Miss Roberta Wellford

This is the side elevation of the design shown on
the previous drawing. Although there is no in-
dication of location or date, if it was a proposal
for 1103 East Main Street in Richmond, then
it must be dated after the war since Rives had
not worked there before.

The drawing is at half the scale of the front
elevation.

Rosz and Son
active ca. 1865

An office building, ca. 1865 (front and side
   elevations)
21 3/16″ x 16 1/2″, pencil and pen and black
   ink with yellow and cream washes on cream
   paper
Scale: 1 inch equals 4 feet
Inscribed, lower center: M. G. Rosz & Son,
   Iron Works | 45 Green Street. | New York
   City.
Owned by the University of Virginia
Ex coll.: Alfred Landon Rives, Miss Landon
   Rives, Miss Roberta Wellford

This drawing was found in the Rives papers,
but since its draughtsmanship differs so much
from that of Alfred Landon Rives, it is assumed that it is an assembly drawing from a sup-
plier of cast-iron fronts for buildings. This
assumption is strengthened by the drawing's inscription. It is further assumed that it is a drawing for a proposed front of a building in Richmond where Rives had opened an office after
the Civil War, and where many such buildings
were being put up.

There is no way to date the drawing exactly
except to suppose it to be post-1865. As a shop
drawing from an ironworks, it is of considerable
rarity.

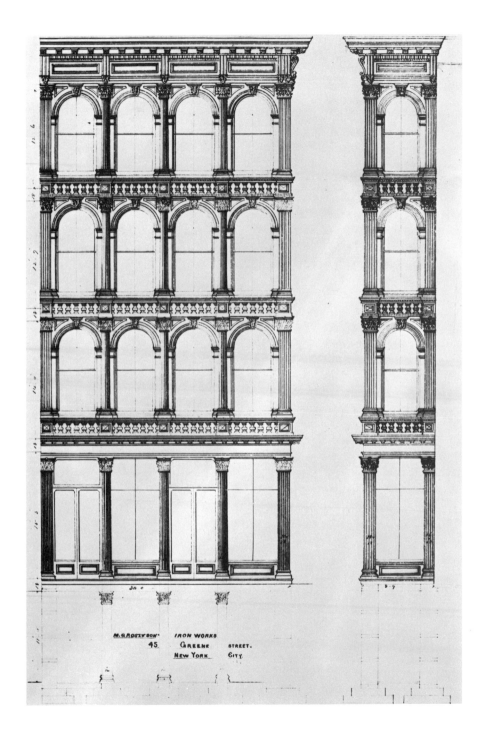

M. G. ROGTVSON. IRON WORKS
45. GREENE STREET.
NEW YORK CITY.

Heinrich and Koch
(Oswald J. Heinrich, active 1846-1866;
Koch, dates unknown)

Richmond, Virginia: Residence for A. Monteiro, 1866 (front elevation)

14 1/2" x 19", pen and black ink and water color on white paper

Scale: 1 inch equals 4 feet

Inscribed, lower center: Front Elevation | of | A. Monteiro's Residence | No. V.

Stamped, lower right: Heinrich and Koch, Architects, Civil and Mining Engineers, Richmond, Va. | Jan. 29, 1866

Owned by the Valentine Museum

Ex coll.: O. X. Heinrich

It is not known whether this design was for Aristides or Andrew Monteiro. Andrew lived at 809 Clay Street between 1866 and 1875, but the house shown in the *Beers Atlas* for 1876 as occupied by Mrs. Monteiro is not the same as that in the drawing. However, since the drawing is labeled "No. V," it might have been an alternate design for the house which was built.

Aristides Monteiro, a doctor, does not seem to have settled in Richmond until well after the date of the drawing.

No information about Koch has been traced.

FRONT ELEVATION
of
A. MONTEIRO'S RESIDENCE
No. V.

Scale 4 feet to an inch.

Elijah E. Myers
1832-1909

Richmond, Virginia: City Hall, 1884 (Elevation)
Pen and ink on linen
Inscribed, lower right: E. J. Myers, archt.
Owned by the City of Richmond

Richmond's City Hall, one of the best extant examples of High Victorian Gothic in the nation, has recently been given a much needed cleaning. It has emerged, as it should, as a Richmond landmark rather than an embarrassment. When it was built, contemporary newspapers not only called it "a gem of architecture" but declared it "evidence of Richmond's progress, prosperity, growth, and ambition."

Its architect, Elijah E. Myers, won the competition for the City Hall on January 4, 1884. He was noted for his public buildings, having designed the old Capitol of the Territory of Utah, now the City and County Building in Salt Lake City, as well as the capitols of Michigan, Colorado, Texas, and Idaho. In addition he won the international competition for the Parliament Buildings in Rio de Janeiro.

Paul Pujol
active 1888

Richmond, Virginia: Pedestal for the Lee
   Monument, 1888 (front elevation)
37 1/4″ x 42 1/4″, pen and black and blue ink
   on linen
Inscribed, upper right: Pedestal Lee Monument
Dated: 25 juin 1888
Signed, lower right: Dressé par l'architecte
   Soussigné | Paul Pujol
   and
   Approuvé | A Mercié
Owned by the Virginia State Library

Although the pedestal for the Lee Monument
on Monument Avenue in Richmond was executed very much as designed, the guardrail with
its pre–Art Nouveau tendencies was never put
in place. At present there is a simple iron fence
made up chiefly of vertical iron rods whose
height obscures the base of the pedestal.

Jean Antonin Mercié (1845-1916) was the
sculptor for the equestrian statue of Lee. Of
Pujol, the architect for the pedestal, no information has been found.

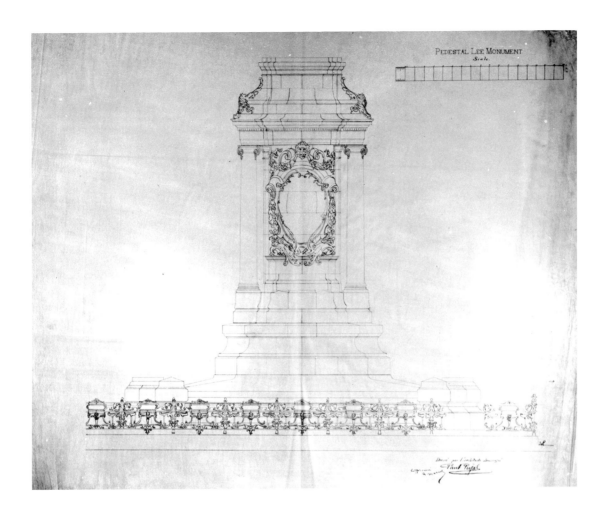

PEDESTAL LEE MONUMENT
Scale.

Dessiné par l'architecte soussigné
approuvé le .... Paul Pujol

M. J. Dimmock
active ca. 1885-1905

Richmond, Virginia: Mortuary chapel, Hollywood Cemetery, ca. 1885-1905 (basement and main-floor plans)

24″ x 37 3/4″, pen and black and scarlet ink on linen

Scale: 1 inch equals 4 feet

Inscribed, upper right: Mortuary Chapel at Hollywood Cemetery | Richmond, Va. | M. J. Dimmock, Architect, | State Bank Building, | Richmond, Va.

Owned by the Virginia State Library

Hollywood Cemetery, begun in 1847, was laid out by John Notman (see p. 26). Its mortuary chapel, however, is a late example of the Gothic Revival. Although not precisely dated, the presence of the rather elaborate plumbing arrangements and the elevator for the corpse indicate that the drawing is probably no earlier than the end of the nineteenth-century.

Unfortunately very little has been discovered about M. J. Dimmock. There is, however, a series of most interesting drawings by him for a variety of buildings, now preserved in the Virginia State Library.

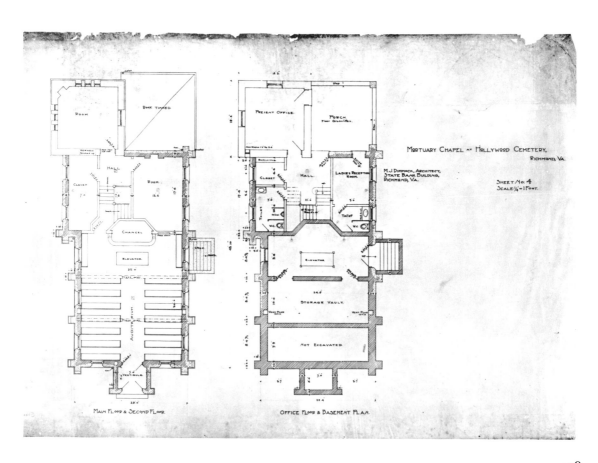

M. J. Dimmock

Richmond, Virginia: Mortuary chapel, Hollywood Cemetery, ca. 1885-1905 (east and north elevations)
18″ x 37″, pen and black ink on linen
Scale: 1 inch equals 4 feet
Inscribed, upper left: Mortuary Chapel at Hollywood Cemetery | Richmond, Va. | M. J. Dimmock, Architect, | State Bank Building, | Richmond, Va.
Owned by the Virginia State Library

The chapel, though later than the original romantic design of the cemetery, fits into the romanticism of its landscape with great ease. Dimmock's sensitivity to this problem and its solution seems all the greater when one realizes that his other extant drawings are designed in the widest possible range of the electicism of the time.

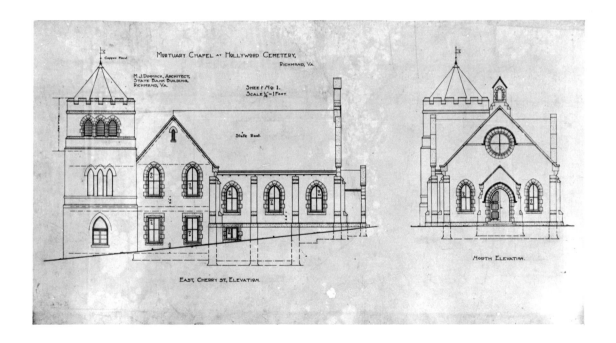

McDonald Brothers
**(Harry P. McDonald, 1848-1904;
Kenneth McDonald, Sr., 1852-1940)**

Charlottesville, Virginia: Proposal for restoration of Rotunda, University of Virginia, 1895-96 (south elevation)
28 1/4" x 32 5/8", pen and black and scarlet ink on white linen
Scale: 1 inch equals 4 feet
Inscribed, upper right: Design For | Restoration of Rotunda | University of Virginia | McDonald Bros. Architects | Scale 1/2"=1 ft Louisville, Ky.
Inscribed, lower center: Front Elevation
Owned by the University of Virginia

On this rejected scheme for the restoration of the burned Rotunda at the University of Virginia, notice the extensive use of metals—cast iron, tin, and galvanized iron for the roof; galvanized iron for the tympanum of the pediment; and cast iron for the door and window surrounds. The columns are fluted, unlike the smooth stucco columns that Jefferson had used. The elevation is dimensioned.

Harry P. McDonald, the elder of the McDonald brothers, was born in Romney, Virginia (now West Virginia), and educated as a civil engineer at Washington and Lee University. He began his career as a railroad construction engineer and was later the superintendent of construction of the Crescent Mill Plant of the Louisville Water Works. He turned to architecture in 1878 and, with his brother, formed the leading architectural firm in Louisville. Their most notable design was, perhaps, the Kansas State Capitol.

Kenneth McDonald, Sr., continued the office after his brother's death in association with William J. Dodd and later with his son Kenneth, Jr.

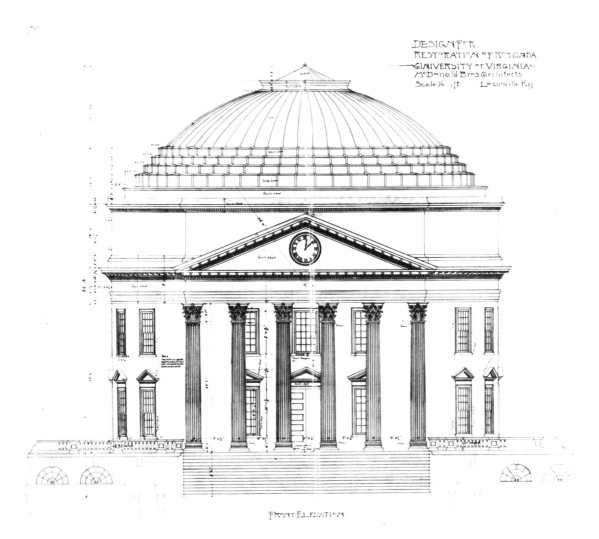

DESIGN FOR
RESTORATION OF ROTUNDA
UNIVERSITY OF VIRGINIA
McDonald Bros Architects
Scale ¼" 1 ft   Louisville Ky

FRONT ELEVATION

III

McDonald Brothers

Charlottesville, Virginia: Proposal for restoration of Rotunda, University of Virginia, 1895-96 (east elevation)

29 1/2″ x 47 3/4″, pen and black and scarlet ink on white linen with some corrections in pencil

Scale: 1 inch equals 4 feet

Inscribed, upper right: Design for | Restoration of Rotunda | University of Virginia | McDonald Bros. Architects | Scale 1/4″ = 1 ft. Louisville, Ky.

Inscribed, lower center: Side Elevation

Owned by the University of Virginia

This east elevation is dimensioned and shows a proposal for a north portico as deep as that on the south. At a smaller scale (1 inch equals 8 feet) a proposed "Esplanade" is shown in elevation stretching to the north and ending with a second monumental flight of steps.

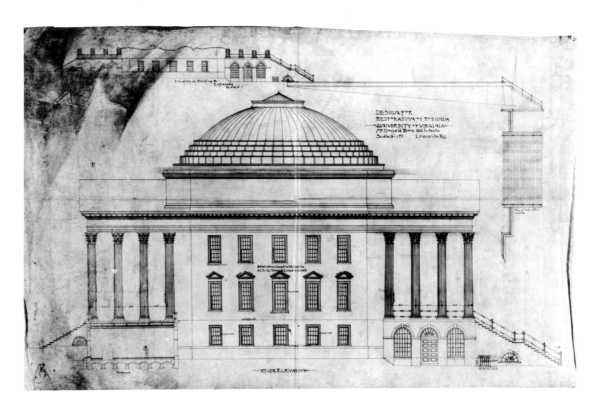

McDonald Brothers

Charlottesville, Virginia: Proposal for restoration of Rotunda, University of Virginia, 1895-96 (section)

28 1/4″ x 41 3/8″, pen and black and scarlet ink on white linen touched with brown and blue washes on reverse

Scale: 1 inch equals 4 feet

Inscribed, top right: Design for | Restoration of Rotunda | University of Virginia | McDonald Bros. Architects | Scale 1/4″ = 1 ft. Louisville, Ky.

Inscribed, lower center: Section A-B

Owned by the University of Virginia

This sectional drawing is dimensioned and contains a good many structural details. Its principal interest, however, is the proposed interior design for the Rotunda with its double dome, its three tiers of orders, its centered statue, and its staircase on the north rather than the south side. Late Victorianism and even a touch of the Art Nouveau have entered into this "restoration" of Jeffersonian classicism.

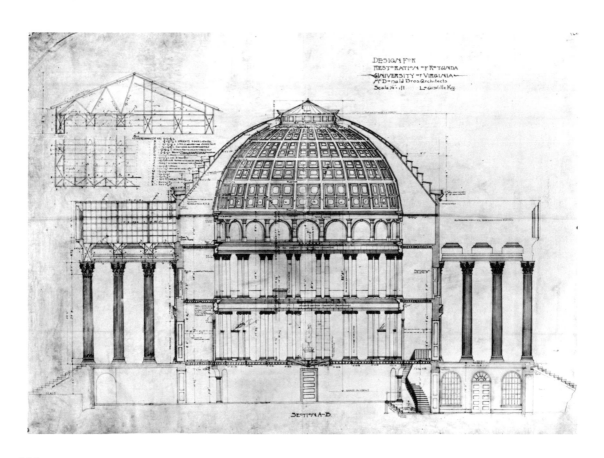

McKim, Mead, and White
(Charles Follen McKim, 1847-1909; William Rutherford Mead, 1846-1928; Stanford White, 1853-1906). Delineator: Hasse

Charlottesville, Virginia: Cocke Hall, University of Virginia, 1896 (partial elevation and section)

36 3/8″ x 30 3/8″, pencil and red ink with blue, green, gray, and pinkish brown washes on detail paper mounted on linen

Scale: 3/4 inch equals 1 foot

Inscribed, lower right: Central Portion of Mechanical Laboratory | University of Virginia | Charlottesville, Va. | McKim, Mead, and White, Archts. 160 Fifth Ave., N.Y. | Scale 3/4″ = 1′-0″

Stamped, lower right: Drawing No. 8 | July 10, 1896 | Made by Haase

Owned by the University of Virginia

Stanford White, who was the member of the firm of McKim, Mead, and White most concerned with the work done at the University of Virginia, was a native New Yorker. As a youth of nineteen he abandoned a preferred career as a painter to be apprenticed as a draughtsman to Henry Hobson Richardson in Boston. It was in that office he met Charles Follen McKim, who had been educated at Harvard and the École des Beaux Arts in Paris.

When White returned from a period of study in Europe in 1879 he was offered a partnership with McKim and Mead, who had been educated at Amherst and had worked and trained with Russell Sturgis. The firm had lost a previous partner who had been McKim's brother-in-law until McKim was divorced. The new firm quickly gained a national reputation and, after the disastrous fire at the University of Virginia in 1895 in the Annex and the Rotunda, was commissioned to restore the Rotunda and design three classroom buildings for the south end of the Lawn.

John Kevan Peebles (see p. 128), an alumnus of the University and a Norfolk architect, made a special trip to the University to suggest Stanford White be employed. The work of the McDonald brothers was then rejected, and White's office carried on with its own designs. In addition to the Rotunda, Rouss, Cabell, and Cocke halls, McKim, Mead, and White also designed Garrett Hall and Carr's Hill for the University.

Charles C. Baldwin, in his book *Stanford White* (New York, 1931), reports that White, speaking of his own projected work for the University of Virginia and of Jefferson's original designs for it, said: "I've seen his plans; they're wonderful: and I'm scared to death" (p. 222). Baldwin further states that "when asked why he did not locate his own buildings nearer to the Jefferson group, White replied that "such temerity must be reserved for a more audacious architect" (p. 322).

This detail drawing of the central pavilion of Cocke Hall (the old Mechanical Laboratory) is dimensioned. Although a note on the drawing points out that the same dimensions and detail serve for the physical laboratory (Rouss Hall), that building was built without the windows shown here.

ELEVATION   CENTRAL PORTION OF MECHANICAL LABORATORY   SECTION
                             UNIVERSITY OF VIRGINIA
NOTE   CHARLOTTESVILLE   VA
SAME DETAIL & DIMENSIONS   McKIM MEAD & WHITE ARCHTS 160 FIFTH AVE N.Y.
FOR PHYSICAL LABORATORY.   SCALE ½"=1'·0"

McKim, Mead, and White
Delineator: Haase

Charlottesville, Virginia: Restoration of Rotunda, University of Virginia, 1896 (south elevation)
22 3/4" x 31 1/4", black ink on linen
Scale: 1 inch equals 1 foot
Inscribed, lower center: Front Elevation | Restoration of Rotunda | University of Virginia | McKim, Mead & White. Architects | 160 Fifth Ave. N. Y.
Stamped, lower right: Drawing No. 8 | April 8, 1896 | Made by Haase
Owned by the New-York Historical Society

The McKim, Mead, and White proposal for the restoration of the Rotunda was the one built. The design is much less Victorian than that by the McDonalds and demonstrates the return to a true classicism which was at that time the new movement.

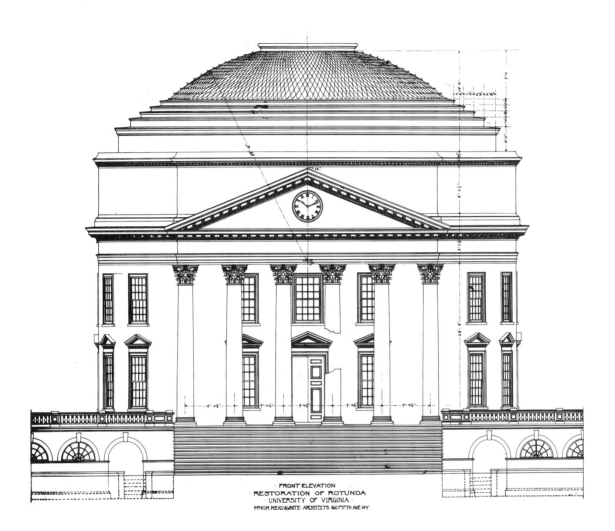

· FRONT ELEVATION ·
RESTORATION OF ROTUNDA
UNIVERSITY OF VIRGINIA
MᶜKIM MEAD & WHITE ARCHITECTS 160 FIFTH AVE NY·

McKim, Mead, and White
Delineator: Haase

Charlottesville, Virginia: Restoration of Rotunda, University of Virginia (east elevation)
26" x 59 1/4", pen and black ink on linen
Scale: 1 inch equals 4 feet
Inscribed, lower center: Side Elevation | Restoration of Rotunda | University of Virginia | McKim, Mead & White. Architects | 160 Fifth Avenue New York
Stamped, lower right: Drawing No. 9 | April 9, 1896 | Made by Haase
Owned by the New-York Historical Society

The new north portico, the new northeast wing, and the new colonnade connecting that and the southeast wing are clearly seen in this drawing.

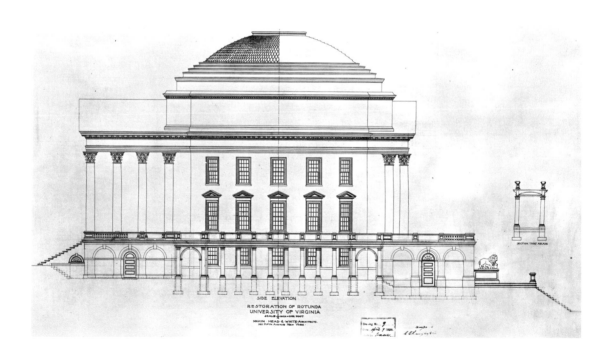

McKim, Mead, and White
Delineator: Haase

Charlottesville, Virginia: Restoration of Rotunda, University of Virginia, 1896 (section)
29 1/4″ x 51″, pen and black ink on linen
Scale: 1 inch equals 4 feet
Inscribed, lower center: Longitudinal Section | Restoration of Rotunda | University of Virginia | McKim · Mead · & · White · Architects | 160 Fifth Avenue New York
Stamped, lower right: Drawing No. 7 | April 9, 1896 | Made by Haase
Owned by the New-York Historical Society

The section shows considerable change from the Rotunda as designed by Jefferson. One floor was abandoned, thus entirely changing the scale of the interior domical space.

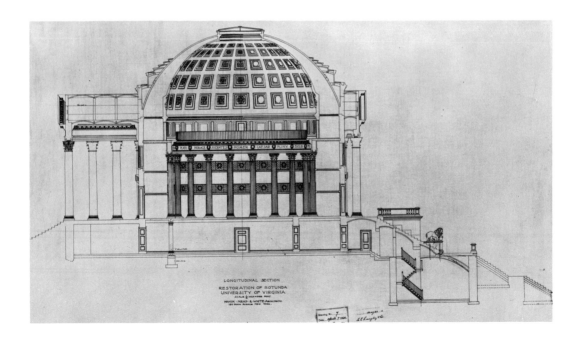

McKim, Mead, and White

Charlottesville, Virginia: Chair for auditorium,
Cabell Hall, University of Virginia, ca. 1896
72 1/2" x 47 3/8", pencil and yellow crayon on
tan tracing paper
Scale: full size
Inscribed, lower right: f. S. D. of Seats in Amphitheatre | Acad. Bldg. University of Virginia | McKim, Mead & White, Archts. | 160 Fifth Ave., N. Y. City
Owned by the University of Virginia

This large drawing of the plan, section, and elevation of one of the chairs in the auditorium of Cabell Hall demonstrates the care with which all the details of the building were designed. The seat and back were bent plywood supported in a cast-iron frame. One of the seats, now no longer used, is included in the exhibition for comparison with the drawing.

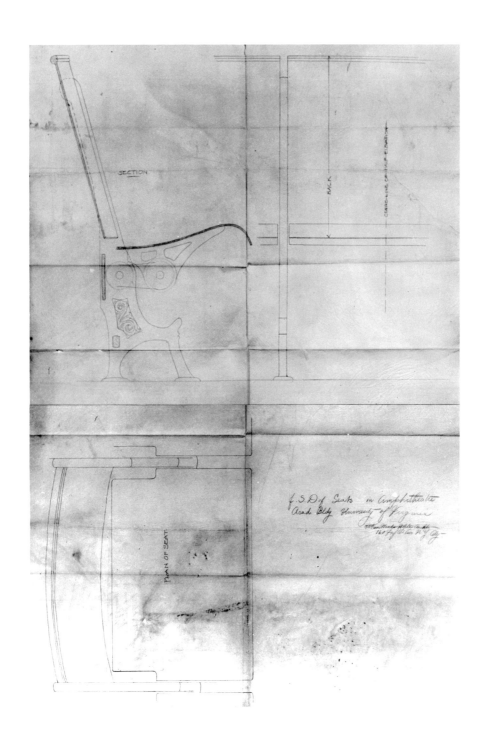

SECTION

BACK

CENTER LINE CAP HALF ELEVATION

PLAN OF SEAT

f. S. D. of Seats in Amphitheatre
Acad Bldg University of Virginia

Alfred Charles Bossom
later Lord Bossom
1881-1965

Richmond, Virginia: Union Bank of Richmond, ca. 1918 (perspective)
21 1/2" x 13 1/2", pencil and black crayon on white paper
Owned by the Valentine Museum

The Exchange Bank of Virginia, designed in 1841 by Isaiah Rogers and built on this site, burned out in the 1865 fire in Richmond. The façade survived and was incorporated in the design of the Union Bank of Richmond, which occupied the site until it was demolished in 1935 to make way for the Parcel Post Annex to the United States Post Office, which had also survived the 1865 fire.

Alfred Charles Bossom was born in London and educated in architecture at the Royal Academy Schools. He came to this country in 1903, staying until 1926 when he returned to England. During that period he produced many buildings, was appointed to the United States Shipping Board, and worked in many states. His commissions in Virginia included the former headquarters building for the Chesapeake and Ohio Railroad in Richmond as well as the bank. During his later years in England he was much engaged in politics, becoming a member of Parliament in 1931, a baronet in 1953, and a life peer in 1960.

Marcellus Eugene Wright
1881-1962

Richmond, Virginia: The Mosque, 1927 (perspective)
34 1/2″ x 43 1/2″, pencil and water color
Signed, lower right: Marcellus E. Wright |
    Charles M. Robinson | Associated Architect
Owned by Marcellus Wright, Jr.

Marcellus Eugene Wright, educated at the University of Pennsylvania, created a successfully exotic building for the Richmond city scape. During the decade of the 1920's such auditoriums were frequently built around the country, but Richmond has retained the best of the extant examples. It still serves as the principal auditorium in the city and also houses the more solemn academic occasions of Virginia Commonwealth University.

Benno Janssen
1874-1964

New Brunswick, New Jersey: House for J.
    Leonard Johnson, 1930 (perspective)
9 3/8" x 20 3/8", pen and black ink on white
    illustration board with dark red and gray
    washes
Inscribed, lower right: Janssen and Cocke,
    Architects, 1930 | House for Mr. J. Leonard
    Johnson, New Brunswick, New Jersey
Owned by Mr. Thomas W. S. Craven

Benno Janssen was educated at the University
of Kansas. His architectural training was gained
in the office of his brother, in the office of Parker
and Thomas in Boston, and in France where he
studied for two years. He returned to Boston but
removed to Pittsburgh in 1905. There he
practiced for three years under the firm name
of Abbot and Janssen, for ten years by himself,
and later under the firm name of Janssen and
Cocke, a firm which executed many of the important educational and residential buildings of
the area. In 1939 he removed to Charlottesville,
Virginia, where he remained, eventually giving
his extensive archiectural library to the University of Virginia.

His drawing shows the extreme skill with
which he arranged the simplest geometric forms
into a romantic and subtle composition. This
skill with the manipulation of simplicity is also
seen in the actual lines of the drawing itself,
which is stripped to essentials but is, at the same
time, richly expressive.

Peebles and Ferguson
(John Kevan Peebles, 1876-1934; Finlay Forbes Ferguson, 1875-1936)

Richmond, Virginia: Virginia Museum, 1932 (elevation)

15 1/4" x 42", pencil and red chalk on white tracing paper

Inscribed, lower center: Virginia Museum of Fine Arts | Richmond, Virginia

Signed, lower right: Peebles and Ferguson, Architects

Owned by the Virginia State Library

In a memorandum dated June 11, 1932, accompanying the drawings for the Virginia Museum, the reliance on daylight from skylights and windows as the principal source of light in a museum building is made very clear. The memorandum said that "the lighting of the building is designed in part as top light and in part as side light in order to meet the varying needs of the exhibits." In the same memorandum it was said that "the design of the structure is that of the English Renaissance of the Wren period. . . . It is believed that this style is appropriate, that it is free from coldness and the reserve of the severely Classic and the somewhat startling character of much of the so called 'Modern.' "

John Kevan Peebles was educated in engineering at the University of Virginia and taught there until 1892. In that year he began the practice of architecture in Norfolk and the following year began work on the first of many buildings for the University, Fayerweather Hall. He was also associated with the design of Minor Hall, Memorial Gymnasium, the Monroe Hill dormitory group, Scott Stadium, McKim Hall, Thornton Hall, and Clark Hall at the University. He was prominent not only in Norfolk but in Richmond, where he was on the committee for the restoration of the Capitol in 1902-3. He

was thus closely linked with two of Jefferson's own designs, the Capitol at Richmond and the University of Virginia. In 1907 he was chairman of the board responsible for the architectural design for the Jamestown Exposition.

Finlay Forbes Ferguson trained at Massachusetts Institute of Technology, beginning his architectural practice about 1890 in Norfolk. By 1917 he was a partner of John Kevan Peebles, and he later served on the Advisory Committee of Architects for the restoration of the historic buildings at Williamsburg.

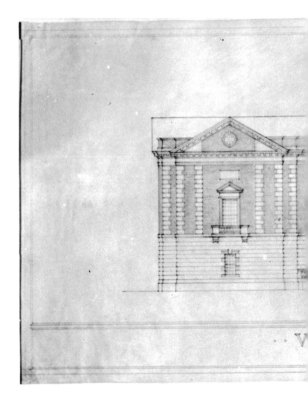

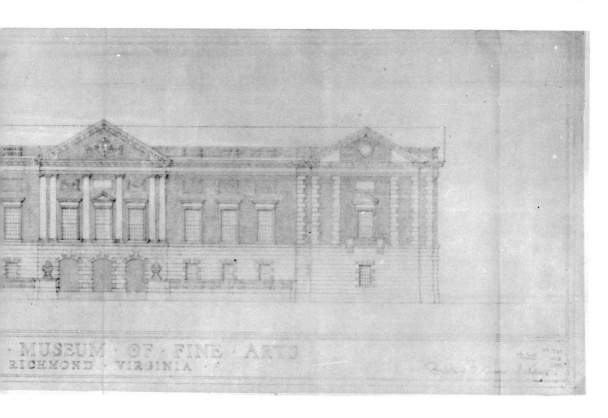

· MUSEUM · OF · FINE · ARTS ·
RICHMOND · VIRGINIA

129

Sidney Fiske Kimball
1888-1955

Charlottesville, Virginia: Tusculum, later called
   Shack Mountain, 1934-35 (proposed site
   plan)
9 5/8" x 10", pencil on tracing paper
Inscribed: House on Shack Mountain | #1 |
   Plot plan. | (not to scale).
Owned by the University of Virginia
Ex coll.: Marie Goebel Kimball

This first site plan for Shack Mountain seems
almost timid compared to the elaboration of the
final design. The well and the existing road are
drawn into the scheme, but the lower terrace
to the north seems to unbalance the plan's
symmetry.

Sidney Fiske Kimball was educated at Harvard and the University of Michigan. In 1916
he issued his *Thomas Jefferson, Architect,* the
result of an interest in Jefferson's architecture
which arose from his studies for his doctorate.
It was an interest he never relinquished, and he
remained the leading scholar of Jefferson's architecture throughout his life.

He founded the School of Architecture at the
University of Virginia during its centennial year,
1919; in 1923 he was appointed chairman of
Fine Arts at New York University; and in 1925
he became the director of the Philadelphia
Museum of Fine Arts.

He retained his affection for Albemarle County and established a vacation house there. It
was called Tusculum at first, but very soon the
name was changed to Shack Mountain. It is
Jeffersonian in character and, in Kimball's time,
was furnished with American period furniture
but hung with a Matisse and a Chirico.

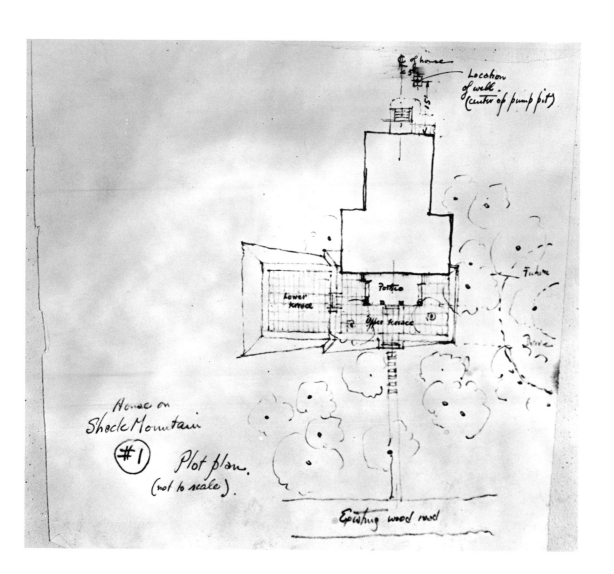

℄ of house
65'

Location
of well
(center of pump pit)

Future

Drive

Lower
terrace

Portico

Upper terrace

House on
Shack Mountain

#1 Plot plan.
(not to scale)

Existing wood road

Sidney Fiske Kimball

Charlottesville, Virginia: Tusculum, later called
    Shack Mountain, 1934-35 (proposed south
    elevation)
18" x 25 1/2", pencil on tracing paper
Scale: 1 inch equals 4 feet
Inscribed: South Elevation, #7
Owned by the University of Virginia
Ex coll.: Marie Goebel Kimball

This first scheme for the house at Shack Mountain was, fortunately, abandoned for the far
more interesting designs seen in the next two
drawings.

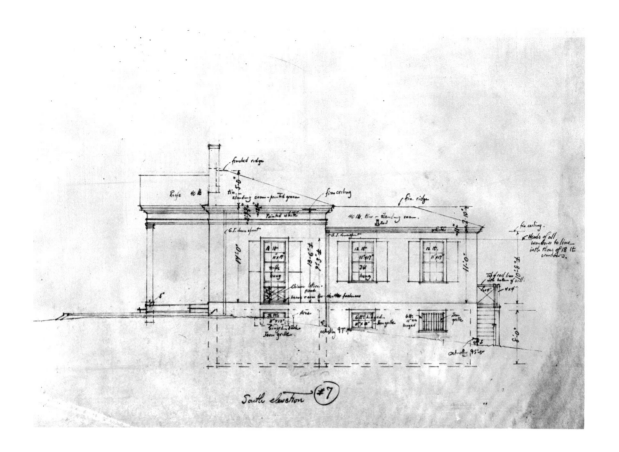

South elevation #7

Sidney Fiske Kimball

Charlottesville, Virginia: Tusculum, later called
Shack Mountain, 1934-35 (site plan, second
scheme)
8 1/2″ x 11″, pencil on onion skin
Inscribed, at right: To establish the plants takes
50 gals each | once a week, or 1000 gals per
day
Owned by the University of Virginia
Ex coll.: Marie Goebel Kimball

This second scheme was largely realized in the
building of Shack Mountain. The T-shaped
house has become semioctagonal at each end of
the crossbar of the T, a device which is at once
more Jeffersonian and more architectonic than
the first scheme.

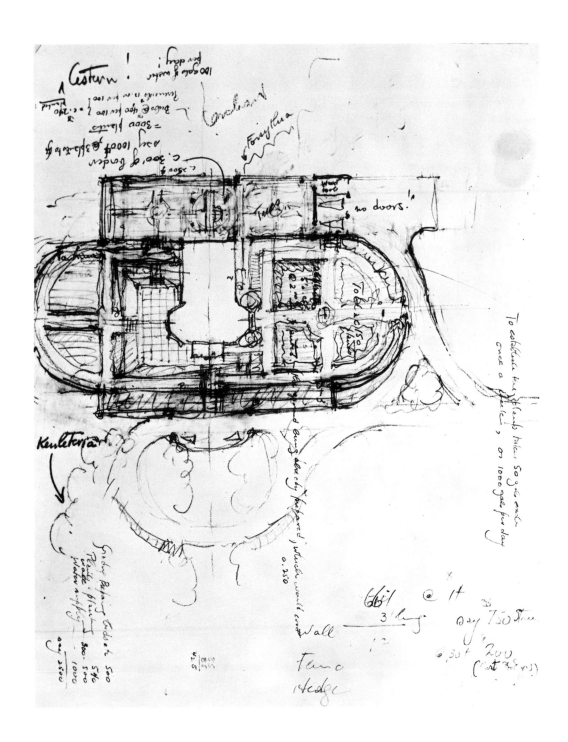

135

Sidney Fiske Kimball

Charlottesville, Virginia: Tusculum, later called
 Shack Mountain, 1934-35 (south elevation
 of second scheme)
11 7/8" x 19", pencil on tracing paper
Scale: 1 inch equals 4 feet
Inscribed: South Elevation, #7
Owned by the University of Virginia
Ex coll.: Marie Goebel Kimball

This elevation shows Shack Mountain about as
it was built. Kimball was so knowledgeable in
the principles of Jeffersonian design that it was
possible for him to create a very convincing
pavilion. In this he was helped by his own attention to detail, backed up by the care of his car-
penters, who at that time still understood the
classic idiom.

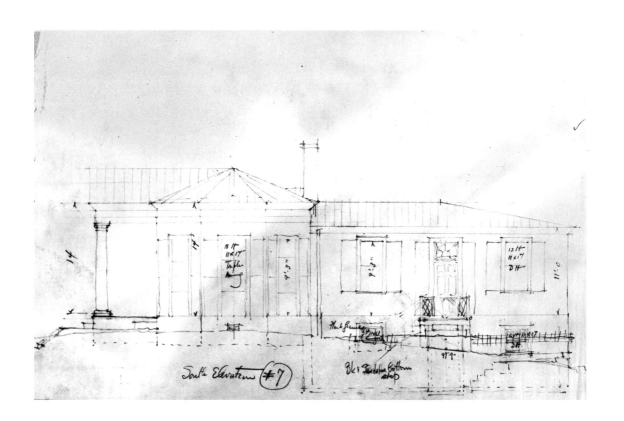

South Elevation #7

Sidney Fiske Kimball

Westmoreland County, Virginia: Studies for
    furniture at Stratford (?): 1. An armchair;
    2. A side table; 3. A candlestand, ca. 1935
1—4 3/8″ x 3 3/4″, pencil on tracing paper
2—2 3/4″ x 4 1/16″, pencil on tracing paper
3—5 5/8″ x 3 3/4″, pencil on tracing paper
Owned by the University of Virginia
Ex coll.: Marie Goebel Kimball

Although there is no positive identification of
these little drawings, it is supposed that they are
studies for the furniture for the restoration of
Stratford, the Lee house in Westmoreland County. Kimball was in charge of the restoration
begun there in 1935. If this furniture was not
for Stratford, it may have been for Shack Mountain.

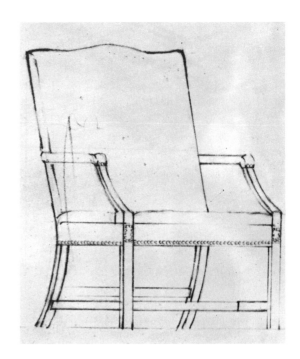

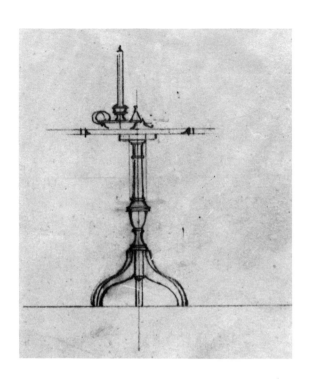

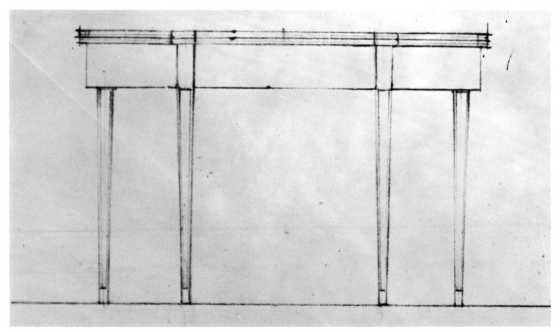

Edmund S. Campbell
1884-1950

Albemarle County, Virginia: Outbuilding at
    Ash Lawn, 1939 (four plans)
21 3/8″ x 35 3/4″, pencil and brown crayon on
    tan tracing paper
Inscribed, lower left: The Quarters at Ashlawn
    —Albemarle Co. | Prelim. study of a plan |
    1/2″=1'-0″ | for Mr. and Mrs. J. Winston
    Johns | Jan. 1939.
Signed, lower center: Edmund S. Campbell,
    Architect
Owned by the University of Virginia

Edmund S. Campbell was trained at Massachusetts Institute of Technology and the École des
Beaux Arts at Paris. He taught at Carnegie Institute of Technology (now Carnegie-Mellon
University) and Armour Institute of Technology
(now Illinois Institute of Technology) and was
the director of the Beaux-Arts Institute of Design in New York before becoming the fourth
chairman of the School of Architecture, University of Virginia, in 1927. He retained this post
until his death in 1950. While serving at the
University, he was also a member of the first
board of advisers for the restoration of Williamsburg. His plan studies for the Quarters at Ash
Lawn, one of Monroe's homes, are labeled:
"No. 1. Presumed original plan founded on all
known information of Jan. 30th 1939."; "No 2.
The most economical proposal"; "No. 3."; and
"No. 4. Very likely the real length of the wood
part."

  It should be noted that the work of such
men as Campbell and Kimball and the work
done at Williamsburg were really pioneering
efforts in preservation, although they took place
no longer ago than the 1930's. Techniques were
explored and experiments tried that have guided
later hands.

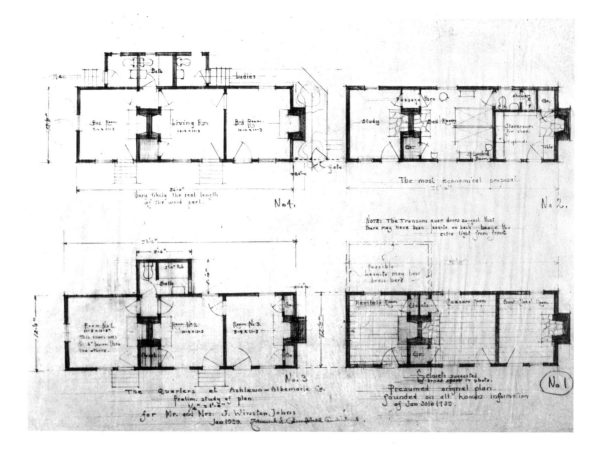

No 4.

Very likely the real length
of the wood part.

The most economical proposal.

NOTE: The Transoms over doors suggest that
there may have been lights on both house the
extra light from front.

No 2.

No 3.

The Quarters at Ashlawn—Albemarle Co.
Prelim. study of plan
1/4" = 1'-0"
for Mr. and Mrs. J. Winston Johns
Jan 1939.

Presumed original plan.
founded on all known information
of Jan 30th 1939.

Closets suggested by broad space in photo.

No 1.

Skidmore, Owings, and Merrill
**(John Ogden Merrill, Sr., 1896——;
Nathaniel Alexander Owings, 1903——;
Louis Skidmore, 1897-1962).
Delineator: Rudolph Associates**

Norfolk, Virginia: Virginia National Bank
    Headquarters Building, 1964 (perspective)
39″ x 26″, pen and black ink and water color
Signed, lower left: Rudolph Assoc. | N. Y. C.
Owned by the Virginia National Bank

Of the state's newer enterprises the consolidation of various banks has been one of the most flourishing. The Virginia National Bank, in need of a new headquarters building, turned to Skidmore, Owings, and Merrill for a design. The drawing captures the riverine spirit of Norfolk, shows the imagination of the Norfolk businessmen, and anticipates the success of the executed building.

Skidmore, Owings, and Merrill is a firm which is peculiarly fitted to grapple with the vast commissions so characteristic of our time. Not only are their buildings gauged to satisfy the needs of their clients, but they never lose sight of the importance of detail and of spirit.

Louis Skidmore was educated at Massachusetts Institute of Technology. He won the Rotch Traveling Fellowship and later worked for Paul Cret and on the Century of Progress Exposition at Chicago, where he met Owings. Owings attended the University of Illinois and Cornell. Skidmore and Owings formed a partnership in 1936. Merrill, who was trained at the University of Wisconsin, the University of Minnesota, and Massachusetts Institute of Technology, joined the firm in 1939.

The firm was associated with Williams and Tazewell and Associates on the commission for the Virginia National Bank.

143

Pier Luigi Nervi
1891————

Norfolk, Virginia: Preliminary Study for The
    Scope, 1966 (general plan)
32″ x 36 1/2″, ozalid print touched with felt
    pen, 1966
Inscribed, upper left: Studio Nervi | Architet-
    tura e tecnica edilizia
Signed, upper left: Pier Luigi Nervi | Antonio
    Nervi
Owned by Williams and Tazewell and Associates

This project at Norfolk, now named The Scope,
will contain a vast underground garage and exhibition hall, as well as a sports arena and a
very large theater–convention hall above ground.

The preliminary study with its off-center
seating shown here has been discarded in favor
of an arena with a centrally placed playing field.

Pier Luigi Nervi was trained in engineering at
the University of Bologna. His work in con-
crete has been one of the major influences in
architecture for several decades. His office now
includes his sons, of whom Antonio was placed
in charge of this project. It is being executed
in collaboration with Williams and Tazewell and
Associates of Norfolk.

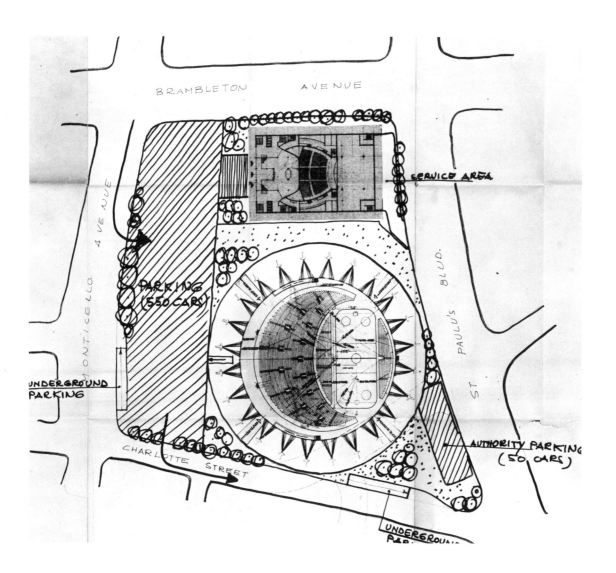

BRAMBLETON AVENUE

SERVICE AREA

MONTICELLO AVENUE

PARKING
(550 CARS)

UNDERGROUND
PARKING

ST. PAULU'S BLVD.

CHARLOTTE STREET

AUTHORITY PARKING
(50 CARS)

UNDERGROUND
PAR...

Pier Luigi Nervi

Norfolk, Virginia: Preliminary Study for the
 Arena of The Scope, 1966 (interior perspec-
 tive)
21″ x 46 1/2″, ozalid print touched with felt pen
Inscribed, upper left: Studio Nervi | Architettura
 e tecnica edilizia
Dated, upper left: May 28, 1966
Signed, upper left: Pier Luigi Nervi | Antonio
 Nervi
Owned by Williams and Tazewell and Associates

This interior perspective shows the dramatic
effect of the off-center seating considered at
one time by Nervi for the arena for The Scope.

Pietro Belluschi (1899———) and Kenneth De May
Delineator: Helmut Jacoby

Charlottesville, Virginia: Architecture Building
    and Fine Arts Library, Fine Arts Center,
    University of Virginia, 1967 (perspective)
17 3/4" x 24 1/2", pencil on tracing paper
Signed, lower left: Jacoby
Owned by Kenneth De May

The first two units of the new Fine Arts Center
at the University of Virginia were completed
during 1969. This drawing, whose viewpoint
is taken from the lowest level of the courtyard,
shows these two units of the Center, the Fine
Arts Library and the School of Architecture.

   The delineator, Helmut Jacoby, has executed
a pencil sketch of great sensitivity and extreme
delicacy which is meant to be strengthened in
values during its photographic reproduction.
The architects for this project are Rawlings and
Wilson with Pietro Belluschi and Kenneth De
May (of Sasaki, Dawson, De May Associates),
the associated architects for design.

148

Index

Aalto, Alvar, xi
Abbot and Janssen, 126
Academy of Design, New York, 86
Albemarle Co., Va., 86, 140-41
Alexandria, Va., 70-71, 86
Amelia Co., Va., 86
American Institute of Architects, Philadelphia Chapter, 26
"Angelo," 40-41
Antique School, New York, 86
Appleton, Thomas, 18, 20
Architects Collaborative, The, xi
Architecture Building, University of Virginia, 148-49
Armour Institute of Technology (now Illinois Institute of Technology), 140
Ash Lawn, 140-41
Aspinwall, James, 44
Augusta, Ga., 32, 60-61
Avery Library, Columbia University, xii, 70

Baldwin, Charles C., 114
Beals, Joseph A., 42-43
Beaux-Arts Institute of Design, New York, 140
Belluschi, Pietro, 148-49
Belmead, Powhatan Co., Va., 86
Bernard, Simon, xi
Bossom, Alfred Charles, Lord, 122-23
Boston, Mass., 70
Boston Athenaeum, 86
Bottomley, William Lawrence, xi
Brady, Josiah R., 86
Breuer, Marcel, xi
Bridge: cast-iron, 66-67; covered, 28-29; masonry, 64
Brockenborough, Arthur S., 2
Brown, Q. H., 28
Brown University, xii, 74
Buckland, William, xi
Business block, 96-99

Cabell Hall, University of Virginia, 114, 120-21
Camden, Caroline Co., Va., 76-79
Campbell, Edmund S., 140-41
Candela, Felix, xi
Capitol: Colorado, 104; Idaho, 104; Kansas, 110; Michigan, 104; Tennessee, 34; Territory of Utah, 104; Texas, 104; Virginia, 82-85, 128; Washington, D. C., 24, 54, 62

Capitol Hill, Richmond, 80
Capitol Square, Richmond, 26; see also Washington Monument
Caroline Co., Va., 76-79
Carnegie Institute of Technology (now Carnegie-Mellon University), 140
Carrère and Hastings, xi
Carr's Hill, University of Virginia, 114
Castle Hill, Va., 34, 62, 72
Chair for auditorium, Cabell Hall, University of Virginia, 120-21
Chambray, Fréart de, 4, 6, 8, 10
Chapel, Laurel Hill Cemetery, Philadelphia, Pa., 26-27
Charleston, S. C., 46
Charlottesville, Va. 2-23, 30-31, 110-21, 126, 130-37, 148-49
Christ Church Rectory, Norfolk, Va., 70
Church of the Redeemer, Baltimore, 76
Cismont, Va., 34-39
Citadel, Charleston, S. C., 46
City Hall, Richmond, 104-5
Clark Hall, University of Virginia, 128
Cobham, Va., 72
Cocke, Gen. John H., 30
Cocke, Col. Philip St. George, 86
Cocke Hall, University of Virginia, 114-15
College of William and Mary, 62
Columbia College, 44
Cornell University, 142
Cottage, White Sulphur Springs, 70
Cram, Ferguson, and Goodhue, xi
Craven, Thomas W. S., xii
Crawford, Thomas, 54-59
Crescent Mill Plant, Louisville, Ky., 110
Cret, Paul, 142
Crozet, Claudius, 28-29

Davis, Alexander Jackson, 86-95
Debtors' Wing, Philadelphia Co. Prison, Moyamensing, Pa., 24-25
De May, Kenneth, xii, 148-49
Dimmock, M. J., 108-9
Dodd, William J., 110

École des Beaux Arts, 114, 140
École Imperiale des Ponts et Chaussées, Paris, 62, 64
École Polytechnique, 28
Exchange Bank of Virginia, Richmond, 122

Fayerweather Hall, University of Virginia, 128
Ferguson, Finlay Forbes, 128-29
Fine Arts Library, University of Virginia, 148-49
First Baptist Church, Richmond, 24
First Presbyterian Church, Baltimore, 76
Ford, G. S., 30-31
Frazee, Architect, 54
Fredericksburg, Va., 44
Freemason Street Baptist Church, 24
Furniture: studies of, for Stratford, 138-39; *see also* Chair

Gale, Robert L., 54
Galt, Alexander, 30
Garrett Hall, University of Virginia, 114
Grace Church, Cismont, Va., 34-39
Green Springs, Va., 86

Haase, delineator, 114, 116, 118, 119
Harrison and Abramovitz, xi
Harvard University, 114, 130
Haviland, John, xi
Headquarters Building, C. & O. Railroad, Richmond, 122
Heinrich, O. X., 32, 60, 102
Heinrich, Oswald J., 32-33, 60-61, 80-81, 102-3
Heinrich and Koch, 102-3
Historical Society of Pennsylvania, xii, 26
Hollywood Cemetery, Richmond, 26, 80-81, 108-9

Ireland, 54

Jacoby, Helmut, 148
Jamestown Exposition, 128
Janssen, Benno, 126-27
Janssen and Cocke, 126
Jefferson, Thomas, xi, 2-21, 22, 30, 82, 114, 128, 130
Johns, Bishop, 70-71
Johnson, J. Leonard, 126-127
Johnson, Philip, xi

Kimball, Marie Goebel, 130, 132, 134, 136, 138
Kimball, Sidney Fiske, 12, 130-39, 140
Kling, Vincent, xi
Koch, Architect, 102

Lantern, Rotunda, University of Virginia, 30-31
Latrobe, Benjamin Henry, xi, 8, 34
Launitz, Architect, 54
Lee, Robert E., xi

Lee Monument, Richmond, 106-7
Leigh, C. J., 70
Leoni, Giacomo, 2, 18
Lexington, Va., 86-95
Louisville, Ky., 110
Lybrock, Albert, 80, 82-85
Lynchburg, Va., 86

MacArthur Memorial, Norfolk, 24
McDonald, Harry P., 110-13, 114
McDonald, Kenneth, Jr., 110
McDonald, Kenneth, Sr., 110-13, 114
McDonald brothers, 110-13, 114
McKim, Charles Follen, 114-21
McKim, Mead, and White, 114-21
McKim Hall, University of Virginia, 128
Makielski, Stanislaw John, v, ix
Massachusetts Institute of Technology, 140, 142
Mead, William Rutherford, 114-21
Memorial Gymnasium, University of Virginia, 128
Mercié, Jean Antonin, 106-7
Merrill, John Ogden, Sr., 142-43
Middle Island Creek, 28-29
Middletown, Va., 86
Mies van der Rohe, Ludwig, xi
Mills, Robert, xi
Minor Hall, University of Virginia, 128
Monteiro, A., residence, Richmond, 102-3
Monteiro, Andrew, 102
Monteiro, Mrs. Andrew, 102
Monteiro, Aristides, 102
Monroe Tomb, Richmond, 80-81
Monticello, 22
Monumental Church, Richmond, Va., 70
Mortuary Chapel, Hollywood Cemetery, Richmond, 108-9
Mosque, Richmond, 124-25
Moyamensing, Pa., 24-25
Myers, Elijah E., 104-5

Nashville, Tenn., 34
Nervi, Antonio, 144, 146
Nervi, Pier Luigi, 144-47
Neutra, Richard, xi
New Bedford, Mass., 70
New Brunswick, N. J., 126-27
New York, 34, 54
New York Historical Society, xii, 116, 118, 119
New York University, 130
Nichols, Frederick Doveton, 12

Norfolk, Va., 24, 142-47,
Notman, John, 26-27, 108

Office building, 100-101
Old Norfolk Academy, Norfolk, Va., 24
Owings, Nathaniel Alexander, 142-43

Palladio, Andrea, 2, 18
Pantheon, 16
Paris, 62
Parker and Thomas, 126
Parliament Buildings, Rio de Janeiro, 104
Pavilion, student drawing for, 32-33
Pavilion II, University of Virginia, 2-3
Pavilion IV, University of Virginia, 4-5
Pavilion VI, University of Virginia, 6-7
Pavilion VII, University of Virginia, 8-9
Pavilion IX, University of Virginia, 22
Pavilion X, University of Virginia, 10-13, 22
Peebles, John Kevan, 114, 128-29
Peebles and Ferguson, 128-29
Pier, design for, 65
Philadelphia, Pa., 26-27, 34
Philadelphia County Prison, 24-25
Philadelphia Museum of Art, 130
Pope, John Russell, xi
Potts, William, 12
Pratt, Mr., 26
Pratt, Richard T., xii, 76, 78, 79
Pratt, Mrs. Richard T., xii, 76, 78, 79
Pratt, William C., 76
Prison, Philadelphia Co., Pa., 24-25
Providence, R. I., 74
Pujol, Paul, 106-7

Railroad station, design for, 68-69, 72-73
Railway carriage, 62-63
Randolph, Cornelia Jefferson, 22-23
Ravenal, Beatrice St. Julien, 46
Rawlings and Wilson, 148
Renwick, James, Jr., 44-45
Renwick, William W., 44
Reservoir, Croton Acqueduct, New York, 44
Residence: in Augusta, Ga., 60-61; of Bishop Johns, 70-71; of J. Leonard Johnson, 126-27; of Sidney Fiske Kimball, 130-37; of C. J. Leigh, 70; of A. Monteiro, 102-3; of William C. Pratt, 76-79; of W. B. Stanard, 70; of VMI faculty, 90-95; of VMI superintendent, 86-89; *see also* individual house names

Richardson, Henry Hobson, 114
Richmond, Va., xi, xii, 24, 32, 40-59, 62, 70, 74-75, 80-85, 86, 96-109, 122-29
Richmond College, 74
Richmond Female Institute, 74-75
Ridgeway, Thomas S., 12
Rives, Alfred Landon, xii, 34, 36, 38, 62-69, 72-73, 96-99, 100
Rives, Miss Landon, 34, 36, 38, 62, 64, 65, 66, 68, 72, 96, 98, 100
Rives, William Cabell, 62
Robinson, Charles M., 124
Rogers, Isaiah, 122
Rogers, Randolph, 54
Rome, 54
Romney, Va., 110
Rosz and Son, 100-101
Rotunda, University of Virginia, xi, 14-21, 22-23, 30-31, 110-19
Rouss Hall, University of Virginia, 114
Royal Academy Schools, London, 122
Royal Institute of British Architects, xii, 24
Rudolph Associates, 142

Saarinen, Eero, xi
St. Patrick's Cathedral, New York, 44
Sands, Joseph, 44
Sasaki, Dawson, De May Associates, 148
School of Architecture, University of Virginia, ix, xi, xii, 148-49
Scope, The, preliminary study for, 144-47
Scott Stadium, University of Virginia, 128
Shack Mountain, Charlottesville, Va., *see* Tusculum
Skidmore, Louis, 142-43
Skidmore, Owings, and Merrill, 142-43
Small, William, xi
Smithsonian Institution, Washington, D. C., 44
Stanard, W. B., 70
Starkweather, Norris G., 76-79
Stieglitz, Christian Ludwig, 14
Stone, Edward D., xi
Stratford, 138-39
Strickland, William, xii, 24, 34-39
Sturgis, Russell, 114
Sturtevant, Philip, 20

Teft, Thomas Alexander, 74-75
Thornton, Dr. William, xi
Thornton Hall, University of Virginia, 128
Thorwaldsen, Architect, 54

Town, Ithiel, 86
Trinity Church, New York, 70
Tusculum (later Shack Mountain) Charlottesville, Va., 130-37

Union Bank of Richmond, 122-23
United States Post Office and Customs House, Richmond, 82, 122
University of Bologna, 144
University of Illinois, 142
University of Kansas, 126
University of Michigan, 130
University of Minnesota, 142
University of Pennsylvania, 124
University of Richmond, 74
University of Virginia, ix, xi, xii, 2-23, 30-31, 34, 36, 62, 64, 66, 68, 72, 96, 98, 100, 110-21, 126, 128, 130, 132, 134, 136, 138, 140, 148-49
University of Wisconsin, 142
Upjohn, Everard, 70
Upjohn, Richard, 70-71

Valentine, Edward V., 32
Valentine Museum, xii, 32, 60, 80, 102, 122
Van de Velde, Henry, xi
Villefranche-sur-Saône, 28
Virginia Commonwealth University, 124
Virginia Military Institute, xii, 28, 62, 86-95
Virginia Museum, ix, 128-29
Virginia National Bank Headquarters Building Norfolk, Va., xii, 142-43
Virginia State Library, xi, xii, 40, 42, 44, 46, 48, 50, 52, 54, 56, 58, 82, 84, 106, 108, 109, 128

Wainwright, Jonathan, Dr., 70
Walker, Francis, 62
Walker, Judith Page, 62
Walter, Thomas Ustick, 24-25
Washington, George, xi
Washington, D. C., 24, 54, 62
Washington and Lee University, 110
Washington Monument, Richmond, xi, 40-59
Welford, Roberta, 34, 36, 38, 62, 64, 65, 66, 68, 72, 96, 98, 100
West Point, N. Y., 28, 46
Westmoreland Co., Va., 138-39
White, Edward B., 46-49
White, Stanford, 114-21
Williams and Tazewell and Associates, xii, 142, 144, 146

Williamsburg, Va., 128, 140
Wipperman, Franziska, 80
Wise, Gov. Henry, 80
Woman's College of Richmond, 74
Wood and Perot, 80
Wren Building, William and Mary, 62
Wright, Marcellus Eugene, 124-25
Wright, Marcellus, Jr., xii

Young, Ammi B., xi

Architectural Drawing in Virginia

was composed, printed, and bound by
Whittet & Shepperson, Richmond, Virginia.
The types are Baskerville, Spartan, and Univers,
and the paper is Mohawk Superfine.
Design is by Edward F. Foss.